# UNWALLED POETRY
*A Different Devotional Experience*

### KIM L. SWEETING

LARGO, MD
USA

Copyright © 2017 Kim L. Sweeting

All rights reserved under the international copyright law. No part of this book may be reproduced or transmitted in any form or by any means, electronic or mechanical, including photocopying, recording, or by any information storage or retrieval system, without express written permission of the author or publisher. The exception is reviewers, who may quote brief passages for review.

Christian Living Books
P. O. Box 7548
Largo, MD 20792
www.christianlivingbooks.com
*We bring your dreams to fruition.*

ISBN Paperback 9781562293123
ISBN Electronic Version 9781562293130

Unless otherwise noted, Scripture quotations are taken from the King James Version of the Bible. Scripture quotations marked (AMPC) are taken from the Amplified Bible®, Copyright©1954, 1958, 1962, 1964, 1965, 1987, by The Lockman Foundation. Used by permission of www.Lockman.org. Scripture quotations marked (AMP) are taken from the Amplified Bible®, Copyright©2015, by The Lockman Foundation. Used by permission of www.Lockman.org. Scripture quotations marked (MSG) are taken from THE MESSAGE. Copyright © by Eugene H. Peterson 1993, 1994, 1995, 1996, 2000, 2001, 2002. Used by permission of NavPress Publishing Group. Scripture quotations marked (NIV) are taken from the Holy Bible, New International Version®, NIV®, Copyright©1973, 1978, 1984, 2011 by Biblica, Inc™ Used by permission of Zondervan. All rights reserved worldwide. www.zondervan.com. Scripture quotations marked (NKJV) are taken from the New King James Version. Copyright© 1982 by Thomas Nelson, Inc. Used by permission. All rights reserved. Scripture quotations marked (NLT) are taken from the Holy Bible, New Living Translation, copyright © 1996, 2004, 2007 by Tyndale House Foundation. Used by permission of Tyndale House Publishers, Inc., Carol Stream, Illinois 60188. All rights reserved.

Printed in the United States of America

# DEDICATION

To my parents, the late Shervin Weldon Thompson and Judith Pamela Thompson, thank you for the foundation you laid in my life that enables me to fly.
I'm forever grateful.

**A Tribute to My Father, the Late Shervin W. Thompson**
**(May 1, 1935 – January 30, 1993)**

Sharp dresser
Health conscious
Eleuthera-born
Really enjoyed life
Very ambitious
Insurance Executive extraordinaire
Naturally sociable

Went for boiled fish on Saturday mornings
Enthusiastically appreciated finer things
Lover of classical music
Dedicated husband, father and grandfather
Optimistic entrepreneur
Never liked to lose Scrabble

Tennis lover, played almost every day
Helped many financially
Only rested occasionally
Methodist Lay Preacher
Playful sense of humor
Served his community and his God
Open to learning
Nimble piano player

*I thank my God upon every remembrance of you.*
(Philippians 1:3)

## A Tribute to My Mother, Judith Pamela Thompson

**J**esus is in her heart
**U**prightness is her goal
**D**edicated to her family and church
**I**nterested in gardening, magazines and her dog
**T**idy, she and dirt are no friends
**H**ealthy, slim and strong

**P**roud of her heritage
**A**dmirable career accomplishments
**M**akes a joyful noise unto the Lord
**E**xemplary lifestyle
**L**aughs a lot, especially at silliness
**A**lways believes in prayer

**T**eacher, never mind her retirement
**H**elpful, always lending a hand
**O**utstanding cook, scrumptiously good
**M**indful of the needs of others
**P**LP, all the way!
**S**urvivor, still standing after many trials
**O**rderly, she likes everything in place
**N**oteworthy mother, and grandmother.

*Favour is deceitful, and beauty is vain: but a woman that feareth the Lord, she shall be praised.* (Proverbs 31:30)

# Contents

| | |
|---|---|
| Foreword | 1 |
| Acknowledgments | 3 |
| Preface | 5 |
| Day 1 – When You Go out Today | 7 |
| Day 2 – It's in the Waiting | 8 |
| Day 3 – Sometimes…Other Times | 9 |
| Day 4 – God's Not Just Looking at the Outside, He's Looking at the Heart | 11 |
| Day 5 – Who Am I? | 13 |
| Day 6 – We Want | 14 |
| Day 7 – Keep Trusting in Him | 15 |
| Day 8 – I Dare You | 17 |
| Day 9 – The Porn Trap | 19 |
| Day 10 – The Price | 21 |
| Day 11 – Align Me Lord | 22 |
| Day 12 – Morning Thoughts of God…Gratitude | 23 |
| Day 13 – The Void | 25 |
| Day 14 – But for God's Grace There Go I | 27 |
| Day 15 – A Place Called Stuck | 29 |
| Day 16 – Remember God Loves You | 31 |
| Day 17 – If You Look to People | 32 |
| Day 18 – Be Careful | 33 |
| Day 19 – Seven-Word Solution to Confusion | 34 |
| Day 20 – An Unfortunately All Too Common Story | 35 |
| Day 21 – Things Are Different…What Happened? | 37 |
| Day 22 – I Need God | 39 |
| Day 23 – What Message Are You Giving to Those You Work With? | 41 |
| Day 24 – Business or Busyness? | 43 |
| Day 25 – What Is More Important to You? | 45 |
| Day 26 – I'm a Kept Woman | 47 |
| Day 27 – Future Worries? | 49 |
| Day 28 – The Blood Is Crying Out | 51 |

| | |
|---|---|
| Day 29 – A Different Kind of Thanks | 53 |
| Day 30 – A Thought about Trust | 55 |
| Day 31 – A Message from a Girl on the Street | 56 |
| Day 32 – The Path to Purpose | 57 |
| Day 33 – Fix Your Gaze upon Me | 59 |
| Day 34 – To the Battle Weary | 61 |
| Day 35 – Good Morning…What a Beautiful Day! | 62 |
| Day 36 – Someone's Standing in the Gap for You | 63 |
| Day 37 – For All the "Mis" People | 65 |
| Day 38 – Transitioning Again | 66 |
| Day 39 – Encouragement for Frustrated Wives | 67 |
| Day 40 – I Am Sovereign | 70 |
| Day 41 – Tonight I Thank God | 71 |
| Day 42 – Don't | 73 |
| Day 43 – Trust Him When You Can't Trace Him | 74 |
| Day 44 – When You Go into Work Today | 76 |
| Day 45 – Be Still | 77 |
| Day 46 – Who Are You Behind Closed Doors? | 78 |
| Day 47 – There's a Place in Your Heart | 80 |
| Day 48 – How to Run On "E" | 81 |
| Day 49 – Rejection…A Gift? | 83 |
| Day 50 – Come Apart | 85 |
| Day 51 – Don't Despair…Hope | 86 |
| Day 52 – Abortion???…An Unborn Child's Plea | 87 |
| Day 53 – For Those Going Through | 89 |
| Day 54 – Beware of Scorn | 90 |
| Day 55 – God Sees and God Knows | 92 |
| Day 56 – Perfect Pastors | 93 |
| Day 57 – Be Still…Again | 95 |
| Day 58 – Eagles Show a Better Way | 97 |
| Day 59 – Morning Haiku | 98 |
| Day 60 – The Sin-Sational Power of Lust | 99 |
| Day 61 – God Loves You | 103 |
| Day 62 – God Can | 104 |
| Day 63 – Thoughts Are Powerful | 105 |

| | |
|---|---|
| Day 64 – Seek Me For Me | 107 |
| Day 65 – Can I Be Honest? | 109 |
| Day 66 – Pow-Her | 112 |
| Day 67 – This Life on Earth Can Be Hard | 113 |
| Day 68 – Grace | 115 |
| Day 69 – To Mothers with a Wayward Child | 116 |
| Day 70 – World Crisis Abounds | 118 |
| Day 71 – God's Law vs. Human Law | 119 |
| Day 72 – To My Children | 120 |
| Day 73 – Challenges?...Believe God | 122 |
| Day 74 – Back to School Encouragement for Students and Teachers | 124 |
| Day 75 – But Can I Trust You? | 126 |
| Day 76 – Are You Anchored? | 128 |
| Day 77 – You or God? | 129 |
| Day 78 – Thought Power | 130 |
| Day 79 – Another Birthday | 131 |
| Day 80 – An in Spite of Praise | 132 |
| Day 81 – Lord Heal the Cracks in My Heart | 134 |
| Day 82 – What Will You Do? –Just Curious | 135 |
| Day 83 – Fiery Trial | 137 |
| Day 84 – Hardheaded Bill | 138 |
| Day 85 – Another Wedding Anniversary | 140 |
| Day 86 – The Zone | 141 |
| Day 87 – Gossip | 143 |
| Day 88 – The Quiet Zone | 144 |
| Day 89 – Still Waiting | 145 |
| Day 90 – Can I Have Some Time with You? | 146 |
| Day 91 – Lord Calm the Raging Storm | 148 |
| Day 92 – Brother George & Pearline | 149 |
| Day 93 – Time for a Re-Think | 151 |
| Day 94 – Another Casualty of Infidelity | 152 |
| Day 95 – A Path to the Promise | 153 |
| Day 96 – Encouragement to Mothers | 156 |
| Day 97 – Hope for the Suicidal | 158 |

| | |
|---|---|
| Day 98 – Lord When It Comes to Prayer Here's the Deal | 163 |
| Day 99 – This Christmas | 165 |
| Day 100 – This Year May Your Christmas Be… | 166 |
| Day 101 – God Is God | 167 |
| About the Author | 168 |

# Foreword

Unwalled, open spaces are wonderful landscapes that invite exploration and discovery. They beckon to us to seek, to venture, to step toward our innate need for more.

*Unwalled Poetry* is a call for the mind to refresh, examine, understand, and to take that quest into new realms of thought.

On your muse through this symphony of words, you will find comfort, counsel and courage. Kim has taken sometimes complex matters and reduced them to concepts that have the power to create character makeovers.

As you read this book, you will hear the voice of one who has been through the crucible of crisis, the office of professional accomplishments, and the school of spiritual instruction.

As a wife, mother, minister, and friend, Kim has shared what has been spoken to her in the Secret Place…the place where there are no walls.

I implore you to go…explore…discover.

Apostle Ricardo "Rick" Dean
Senior Pastor
Family of Faith Ministries International
Nassau, Bahamas
www.familyoffaithintl.org

# Acknowledgments

First and foremost to God, my Heavenly Father…I thank and praise You for who You are to me, for all You've done for and through me, and for the birthing and completion of this book, a ministry tool that I pray You will work through to touch lives all around the world for Your honor and glory and the advancement of Your Kingdom.

To my husband Joe…thank you for your love and for your patient support in this, and all my endeavors. I love and appreciate you.

To my children, Joseph, Joel, and Esther, my priceless, unique gifts whom I love…thank you for your support and encouragement…special thanks to Joel for always being ready and willing to give "on point" feedback.

To my Pastor, Apostle Ricardo A. C. Dean, Senior Pastor of Family of Faith Ministries International, Nassau, Bahamas…thank you for consenting to write the Foreword and for the rich multifaceted deposits you've made in my life over the past 17 years.

To Tiffany Edgecombe ("Tiff"), bestselling author of *A Time to Heal – Restoration from the Ravages of Rape and Overcoming Obstacles – A Fight to the Finish*…thank you for your encouragement and informative input regarding the publishing process.

To my friend Rhonda…thank you for telling me so many times over the years that whenever you go into a bookstore, you see my books on the shelves…by God's grace this is the first one girl!

To the followers and visitors of my blog, "Unwalled" and the persons on my email list…your feedback of how God touches your lives through my writing inspires me to continue on…thank you. (www.unwalled.wordpress.com)

To you…thank you for investing in your spiritual growth and development through the purchase of *Unwalled Poetry*…may multiplied blessings be upon you as you read.

# Preface

In February of 2010, I started a blog called "Unwalled" to encourage, edify, and inspire the Body of Christ in the Bahamas and beyond.

To vary my blog's content, I occasionally posted original poems birthed out of my own experiences as well as those of others that spoke to various spiritual, personal, and social issues in an easy-to-read relatable way. The result was that God used the poems to minister to and bless the lives of persons all around the world. *Unwalled Poetry* is a collection of poems from "Unwalled" compiled in one volume just for you.

Apart from its content, what makes this book unique is that unlike other poetry books, it is specially formatted for you to read and meditate on one poem and its related scripture a day, making it a different and exciting devotional. After reading each poem and scripture, I invite you to reflect on and answer the following two questions:

1. What do you believe God is speaking to your heart?
2. How will you apply this revelation to your life?

Taking this additional step will further enrich your devotional experience, challenge you to a deeper walk with the Lord and increase your spiritual growth.

*Unwalled Poetry* also works well as a group devotion/discussion tool. A poem and accompanying scripture can be chosen for the group to read, then each person can share what they believe God is saying to them and how they plan to apply the revelation to their life.

It is my prayer that God uses my poems to encourage your heart, edify your spirit, and inspire your soul…that He uses them to lead you into a richer, deeper, fuller relationship with Him and with others…that He uses them to birth indelible change in your life for His honor and glory.

Abundant Blessings,
Kim

# Day 1
## WHEN YOU GO OUT TODAY

When you go out today,
Go with the knowledge that you are a child of the Most High God,
Go with the knowledge that the Holy Spirit is in you,
Go with the knowledge that angels are encamped round about you,
Go with the knowledge that you are not alone.

When you go out today,
Go with the knowledge that your day is not a mystery to your Father,
Go with the knowledge that His wisdom is just a prayer away,
Go with the knowledge that His power lays within you,
Go with the knowledge that there is nothing He won't enable you to face.

When you go out today,
Go with the knowledge that the joy of the Lord is your strength,
Go with the knowledge that no weapon formed against you shall prosper,
Go with the knowledge that you are more than a conqueror through Christ Jesus,
Go with the knowledge that it's about His Kingdom, it's not about you.

When you go out today,
Go with the knowledge that this world is not your home,
Go with the knowledge that your citizenship is in heaven,
Go with the knowledge that you are on assignment,
Go with the knowledge that you are just passing through.

*Scripture*   *My people are destroyed for lack of knowledge.* (Hosea 4:6)

# Day 2
## IT'S IN THE WAITING

........................................

It's in waiting on the Lord that we gain an understanding of His Word,
It's in waiting on the Lord that we get to learn His ways,
It's in waiting on the Lord that our spirit is strengthened,
It's in waiting on the Lord that our flesh is mortified.

It's in waiting on the Lord that the true motives of our hearts are revealed,
It's in waiting on the Lord that we receive rhema words from on High,
It's in waiting on the Lord that His will for our lives is clarified,
It's in waiting on the Lord that we recognize our total and utter dependence on His Being.

It's in waiting on the Lord that our spirit is sustained,
It's in waiting on the Lord that our character is built,
It's in waiting on the Lord that discipline is fostered,
It's in waiting on the Lord that hope is kept alive.

It's in waiting on the Lord that we are filled with His power,
It's in waiting on the Lord that we receive His direction,
It's in waiting on the Lord that our prayer life increases,
It's in waiting on the Lord that we grow in our trust in Him.

It's in waiting on the Lord that we are prepared to be effective Believers in this world, advancing the Kingdom of God and demonstrating His glory in all facets of our lives.

It's in the waiting on the Lord.

*Scripture*   I wait for the Lord, I expectantly wait, and in His word do I hope.                    (Psalms 130:5 AMPC)

## Day 3
### SOMETIMES...OTHER TIMES

Sometimes our prayers are like dynamite, explosively changing our situations with results easily seen.
Other times they are like a constant drip of water on a rock, steadily eroding the dynamics of our situation with changes hidden from the naked eye.

Sometimes healing manifests in our bodies instantly, miraculously, effortlessly.
Other times it is a painstaking process entailing physical suffering and requiring continuous faith until manifested promise.

Sometimes God gives us the very thing that we want.
Other times like a loving parent, He withholds it for our own good.

Sometimes we pray that a person lives through a life-threatening situation and they survive.

Other times we pray fervently, believing for them to live and they die.

Sometimes provision comes for financial needs way in advance.
Other times it comes on the 59th minute of the 11th hour.

Sometimes God delivers us from fiery trials.
Other times we have to walk through the fire of affliction from beginning to end.

But rest assured that at all times God has our best interests at heart so we can trust Him.

*Scripture*   *And we know that God causes everything to work together for the good of those who love God and are called according to his purpose for them.*                    (Romans 8:28 NLT)

# Day 4

## GOD'S NOT JUST LOOKING AT THE OUTSIDE, HE'S LOOKING AT THE HEART

His words came across with great passion and flair,
Electricity and excitement filled the air,
He had unquestionably mastered preaching as an art,
But God's not just looking at the outside, He's looking at the heart.

Her voice was melodious oh what a delight,
She sung out those words with all of her might,
No doubt she was the right choice for the part,
But God's not just looking at the outside, He's looking at the heart.

The program went beautifully the children all came,
Hot dogs, drinks, chips and a beautiful game,
Bible stories were presented on eye-catching charts,
But God's not just looking at the outside, He's looking at the heart.

Every house was visited in the neighborhood that day,
Absolutely nothing or no one got in the way,
The outreach team moved with precision like a well-aimed dart,
But God's not just looking at the outside, He's looking at the heart.

The service was planned the special guests came,
Excellence was definitely the name of the game,
Everything went perfectly right from the start,
But God's not just looking at the outside, He's looking at the heart.

My fellow Ambassadors remember each day,
It's important to search our motives and pray,
Our deeds may seem good, worthy and sweet as a tart,
But God's not just looking at the outside, He's looking at the heart.

*Scripture*   The LORD does not look at the things man looks at. Man looks at the outward appearance, but the LORD looks at the heart.

(1 Samuel 16:7)

## Day 5
### WHO AM I?

I am so powerful yet I am so sly,
I play you like a fool so you hold your head high,
Through me you despise others looking at them down your nose,
Through me you speak ill about and make fun of their clothes.

I am the force who makes you sit still and falter
When the Spirit of God bids you come to the altar,
I subtly whisper, "you're always right"
So you ignore all advice to my utter delight.

I urge "don't say sorry", "don't apologize",
And you foolishly listen to your demise,
Hey, hide all your problems keep them safe and sound,
That's how I know you'll definitely remain bound.

Rely on yourself you don't need help to do it,
Ha! Now you're flat on your face, wow you're so stupid!
You hearken to me at my every call and beck,
Good! That empowers me to keep my foot on your neck.

Okay, I'll reveal myself no longer will I hide,
I'm a stronghold in your life my name is pride.

*Scripture*  *Pride goes before destruction, a haughty spirit before a fall.*
*(Proverbs 16:18 NIV)*

# Day 6
## WE WANT

We want to reap, but not to sow...
We want to get, but not to give...
We want the crown, but not the cross...
We want forgiveness, but not to forgive...

We want to be exalted, but not to humble ourselves...
We want the "promised land", but not the wilderness...
We want the power, but not the obedience...
We want to preach, but not to study...

We want the anointing, but not to pay the price for it...
We want deliverance, but not repentance...
We want to be content with much, but not to be content with little...
We want God's "yes", but not His "no" ...

We want Kingdom principles, but not the King of the principles...
We want His hand, but not His face...
We want His purpose, but not His process...
We want to reign with Him, but not to suffer with Him...

We want to have His life, but not to lose our life...
We want Him as Savior, but not as Lord...
We want the talk, but not the walk...
We want God on our terms not on His.

Beloved, do not be deceived; this will never work!

*Scripture*  *And he said to them all, If any man will come after me, let him deny himself, and take up his cross daily, and follow me.*

*(Luke 9:23)*

# Day 7
## KEEP TRUSTING IN HIM

...........................................

When your best friend lets you down...keep trusting in Him.
When no one calls or comes around...keep trusting in Him.
When your heart's about to break...keep trusting in Him.
When there's not much more you can take...keep trusting in Him.

When unexpectedly things go gravely wrong...keep trusting in Him.
When you can't even muster up a song...keep trusting in Him.
When your deepest dream seems to have died...keep trusting in Him.
When you're crushed and bleeding with pain inside...keep trusting in Him.

When the funds are simply just not there...keep trusting in Him.
When people look down their noses and sneer...keep trusting in Him.
When healing seems to be on hold...keep trusting in Him.
When your spouse is acting cold...keep trusting in Him.

When it seems there's absolutely no way out...keep trusting in Him.
When you're plagued with fear and doubt...keep trusting in Him.
When your enemies laugh and seem to win...keep trusting in Him.
When you're battling intensely with besetting sin...keep trusting in Him.

When the questions run oh so deep...keep trusting in Him.
When you can't even get a good night's sleep...keep trusting in Him.
When it seems all glimmer of hope is gone...keep trusting in Him.
When you feel you just can't go on...keep trusting in Him.

No matter what you face...keep trusting in Him.
By grace you can complete this race...keep trusting in Him.
Hold tight the end is very near...keep trusting in Him.
Press on in effectual fervent prayer...keep trusting in Him.

Keep trusting in Him.

*Scripture*    *Those who trust in the LORD Are like Mount Zion, which cannot be moved, but abides forever.*    (Psalms 125:1 NKJV)

## Day 8
### I DARE YOU

..................................................

*I* dare you to stop focusing on whatever you don't have and start thanking God for what you do have.

I dare you to prioritize regular time alone with God, meditating on His Word and communing with Him.

I dare you to obey the Lord re: your finances and give as He directs you to give.

I dare you to trust God's love, wisdom, and timing with His purposes and plans for your life instead of stressing yourself out trying to make things happen in your way and your time.

I dare you to honor the marriage covenant you made before the Lord and not have that extra-marital affair you are considering.

I dare you to do that thing that you know is necessary to improve your relationship with your spouse and children.

I dare you to stop being more concerned about what others think than you are about what God thinks; to purpose to be a God-pleaser and not a man-pleaser.

I dare you to bless your enemies and to pray for the persons who despitefully use you.

I dare you to practice walking in integrity, to express a "yes" on the outside only if there is a "yes" on the inside, and to express a "no" on the outside only if there is a "no" on the inside.

I dare you to sincerely ask God to set you free from that pleasurable "secret" sin that binds you and keeps you from fully committing your life to Him and walking in your Kingdom purpose.

I dare you to honor your father and your mother in spite of their wrongdoing, failures and shortcomings.

I dare you to forgive that person who hurt you, so, so deeply, and thereby set yourself free to experience the needed healing in your life.

I dare you to take God at His Word concerning every area of your life, to adopt a "God said it, I believe it, that settles it" attitude always.

I dare you.

*Scripture*    *Let us think of ways to motivate one another to acts of love and good works.*    (Hebrews 10:24 NLT)

# Day 9

## THE PORN TRAP

........................................

In the middle of the night when your spouse is asleep,
To the computer you would quietly creep,
A press of a button a few clicks of a mouse,
Who are these strangers you are letting in your house?

The screen comes alive with bodies galore,
Every kind of image you can think of and more,
Clothing all absent everything spread,
Your body heats up as sights sink in your head.

Some hours later you're still glued to the screen,
Now you're feeling anything but clean,
Your bodily fluids are all over you,
Is this really what you want to do?

You sneak back to bed and under the quilt,
Now you're laden down with all kinds of guilt,
The images permeate your mind through and through,
You're finished with them, but they're not finished with you.

You try to play tough you try to play strong,
You try to convince yourself you've done nothing wrong,
But my brother, my sister there's something deathly wrong with that,
Once you've looked on with lust you've committed the act.

Whether or not you want to admit it,
You're bound up in sin and you need to quit it,
The enemy has a vice-like grip on you,
And it's only God's power that can bring the breakthrough.

You're not just reading this because it is near,
It's God's Spirit speaking to you loud and clear,
He's saying my son, my daughter, come running to me,
I love you, I'll forgive you, I'll set you free.

So stop sneaking, stop hiding, stop pretending today,
Instead humble yourself on your knees and pray,
A broken heart and contrite spirit He will not despise,
With His help from these ashes you shall arise.

*Scripture*  But I say, anyone who even looks at a woman with lust in his eye has already committed adultery with her in his heart.
(Matthew 5:28 NLT)

# Day 10
## THE PRICE

The price of the anointing is obedience.

The price of obedience is self-denial and sacrifice.

The price of self-denial and sacrifice is a desire to do My will.

The price of a desire to do My will is your love for Me above all else and that is what I require from you.

Will you pay the price?

Selah!

*Scripture*    *Then Jesus said to His disciples, "If anyone desires to come after Me, let him deny himself, and take up his cross, and follow Me.*
(Matthew 16:24 NKJV)

# Day 11
## ALIGN ME LORD

........................................................

Align me Lord
Align my will with Your will
Align my thoughts with Your thoughts
Align my words with Your words
Align my motives with Your motives
Align my plans with Your plans
Align my desires with Your desires
Align my steps with Your steps
Align my goals with Your goals
Align my dreams with Your dreams
Align me Lord

*Scripture*  Can two walk together, except they be agreed? (Amos 3:3)

# Day 12

## MORNING THOUGHTS OF GOD…GRATITUDE

························································

This morning I thought of how blessed I am to have the privilege of being one of God's children because of my belief, faith and trust in Jesus Christ as my Savior and Lord,

Of how when I pray, I can call Him, the God who spoke this universe into existence by the creative power of His Word, "Father" and know that He hears my prayers,

Of how in all of His glory, majesty, dominion, power, and holiness, He is still mindful of me and concerned about every detail of my life, even to the extent of numbering the very hairs on my head.

This morning I thought of how God's grace, His divine favor and enabling power is ever present in my life to help me to do and be all that He desires me to do and be, and I do not have to rely on my limited human strength,

Of how when I sin, when I miss the mark and fall short of His standard and glory, once I confess it with a repentant heart, He forgives me and cleanses me from all unrighteousness and removes that sin as far away as the east is from the west and remembers it no more,

Of how when I am in need of wisdom, all I have to do is ask Him and by His Holy Spirit He freely gives it to me and lets me know how best to navigate through any circumstance.

This morning I thought of how in spite of the danger and terror that plagues the earth, I can rest in knowing that He is the divine protection over my life, that He is my shield and my defense and His angels encamp around me to guard me,

Of how whenever others reject me, it's okay because I have laid hold of the truth that He accepts me through Christ and that acceptance is most important, satisfying and priceless,

Of how He has a plan for my life and even if it does not feel like it, or even if I can not see it, He is working all things in my life together for good because I love Him and I have been called according to His divine purpose.

This morning I thought of how He formed me and knit me together in my mother's womb and in His eyes I am a fearfully and wonderfully made designer's original so the world's standards of external beauty really do not matter,

Of how I am never alone because His Spirit dwells within me, and He promised never to leave me nor forsake me,

Of how He loves me with an incomprehensible, unfathomable, mind-blowing love that nothing can separate me from.

This morning I thought of how blessed I am to have the privilege of being one of God's children because of my belief, faith and trust in Jesus Christ as my Savior and Lord.

And I was overwhelmed with gratitude.

*Scripture*  *O give thanks to the Lord, for He is good; for His mercy and loving-kindness endure forever!*
 (Psalms 107:1, 118:1, 136:1 AMPC)

# Day 13

## THE VOID

You've got the cool car, the job, the promotion,
You've got the degree and the house by the ocean,
You've got the new spouse and baby too,
But there's something still missing inside of you.

You hang with the "in crowd" you're "stylin" straight through,
When it comes to the latest no one can touch you,
Clothes, hair, cell phone, music, whatever it may be,
You've got it going on but you're still unhappy.

In the middle of the night the questions run deep,
How come I have all of this and can't even sleep?
I have everything I want and in which I delight,
But I'm empty inside so I can't be alright.

Now it's not only at night but at daytime too,
The questions and discomfort are really bugging you,
Outside praise for your lifestyle continues to flow,
But deep on the inside you're ready to blow.

Frantically you search and call out with a plea,
Who or what on this earth can deliver me?
I've done all I can think of and I'm still a mess,
And the worse thing of all is people think I'm so blessed.

Hey my brother, my sister, listen up and don't doubt,
It's that God created void that's beginning to shout,
In His love, mercy, grace and sovereign will,
He's reserved a space in you that only He can fill.

It's His Holy Spirit that's been tugging at your heart,
Only a relationship with God will satisfy that empty part,
Receive Jesus Christ as your Savior and Lord today,
And all of that inner nagging will vanish away.

It may not seem "off the chain" "hip" or "all that" but you see,
It's the only proven, tried, true and sure remedy,
So please don't hesitate whatever you do,
He's here today patiently waiting just for you.

*Scripture*   For he satisfieth the longing soul and filleth the hungry soul with goodness.    (Psalm 107:9)

# Day 14

## BUT FOR GOD'S GRACE THERE GO I

........................................

The barbershop was filled with men fat and thin,
They laughed and made fun of how this guy got turned in,
"He's been stealin from his job for years" was the cry,
Ray said, but for God's grace there go I.

Walking through the mall was a company of three,
Tongues wagging fast, faces lit up with glee,
"Humph! Singing in the choir now her belly puff up high",
Cindy said, but for God's grace there go I.

At the luncheon today many people were there,
Harsh words about the fallen preacher filled the air,
"He should know better", "He deserves to die",
Phil said, but for God's grace there go I.

In the cafeteria at work some ladies were squawking,
Near the water cooler another crew were gawking,
"Das good, he too slick an he too like to lie",
Bernice said, but for God's grace there go I.

Ray, Cindy, Phil and Bernice are all very wise,
They look at other's faults through humble eyes,
Whenever they learn what someone else has done,
They're not quick to judge and hold out a gun.

So if you hear of a person who takes a great fall,
Before commenting from a high horse check your life first of all,
For if you are honest you too will sigh,
And say but for God's grace there go I.

*Scriptures* Judge not, that you be not judged. For with what judgment you judge, you will be judged; and with the measure you use, it will be measured back to you. (Matthew 7:1-2 NKJV)

*Brothers, if anyone is caught in any sin, you who are spiritual [that is, you who are responsive to the guidance of the Spirit] are to restore such a person in a spirit of gentleness [not with a sense of superiority or self-righteousness], keeping a watchful eye on yourself, so that you are not tempted as well.*
(Galatians 6:1 AMP)

*So, if you think you are standing firm, be careful that you don't fall!*
(1 Corinthians 10:12 NIV)

# Day 15
## *A PLACE CALLED STUCK*

........................................

Have you ever been in a place called stuck?

A place where walls seem insurmountable,
Rivers seem uncrossable,
Ideas seem impossible.

Have you ever been in a place called stuck?

A place where nothing seems to be moving,
Everything seems to be at a standstill,
Spinning your wheels seems to be the norm.

Have you ever been in a place called stuck?

A place where doors seem closed,
Windows seem locked,
Options seem shot.

Have you ever been in a place called stuck?

A place where efforts seem fruitless,
Passion seems fireless,
Progress seems only a dream.

Have you ever been in a place called stuck?

A place where prayers seem to hit the ceiling,
Praise seems void of power,
Worship seems lifeless and routine.

Have you ever been in a place called stuck?

A place where God seems to be absent,
The devil seems to be dominating,
Hope seems lost.

Have you ever been in a place called stuck?

Hold on...it's not what it seems...this too shall pass.

*Scripture*  *To everything there is a season, a time for every purpose under heaven.* (Ecclesiastes 3:1 NKJV)

## Day 16
### REMEMBER GOD LOVES YOU

When you don't know what to do,
When the news just can't be true,
When you're feeling sad and blue,
Remember God loves you.

When everything comes crashing down,
When friends and loved ones can't be found,
When mental chains have you bound,
Remember God loves you.

When crisis comes with all its clout,
When you just want to scream and shout,
When no matter what, you can't figure it out,
Remember God loves you.

When lifelong dreams evade your touch,
When you feel it's simply just too much,
When gripped by sorrow your chest you clutch,
Remember God loves you.

When your path is hard and rough,
When situations are oh so tough,
When you've simply had enough,
Remember God loves you.

Remember God loves you!

*Scripture*   *I trust in God's unfailing love for ever and ever.*
                                            (Psalms 52:8b NIV)

# Day 17

## IF YOU LOOK TO PEOPLE

••••••••••••••••••••••••••••••••••••••••••••••••

If you look to people to be what only God can be in your life,
You will be disappointed.

If you look to people to do what only God can do in your life,
You will be disappointed.

If you look to people to solve what only God can solve in your life,
You will be disappointed.

If you look to people to change what only God can change in your life,
You will be disappointed.

If you look to people to fill what only God can fill in your life,
You will be disappointed.

If you look to people to ease what only God can ease in your life,
You will be disappointed.

If you look to people to heal what only God can heal in your life,
You will be disappointed.

So don't look to people,

Look to God.

*Scripture*   Cursed is the man who trusts in man and makes flesh his strength, Whose heart departs from the Lord. Blessed is the man who trusts in the Lord, and whose hope is the Lord.

(Jeremiah 17:5, 7 NKJV)

## Day 18
### BE CAREFUL

...........................................

*B*e careful.

Be careful not to allow
the pressure of expectations,
the lack of understanding,
the looks of disapproval,
the negative vibes,
the critical spirit,
the absence of support,
the wary facial expressions,
the scorn,
the gossip,
the threats,
from those around you,
and even closest to you,
to cause you to divert from or abandon
the path,
the process,
and ultimately,
the fulfillment
of what you know to be God's will for your life.

Be careful.

*Scripture* Let your eyes look right on [with fixed purpose], and let your gaze be straight before you. Consider well the path of your feet, and let all your ways be established and ordered aright.

(Proverbs 4:25-26 AMPC)

# Day 19

## SEVEN-WORD SOLUTION TO CONFUSION

••••••••••••••••••••••••••••••••••••••••••

**STOP**
what you are doing

**LOOK**
to the Lord for direction

**LISTEN**
for His voice

**WAIT**
until He speaks

**HEAR**
what He tells you

**PROCEED**
and do what He says

**REPEAT**
as necessary.

*Scripture* — If any of you lacks wisdom, you should ask God, who gives generously to all without finding fault, and it will be given to you. But when you ask, you must believe and not doubt, because the one who doubts is like a wave of the sea, blown and tossed by the wind. That person should not expect to receive anything from the Lord. (James 1:5-7 NIV)

# Day 20
## AN UNFORTUNATELY ALL TOO COMMON STORY

Pastor devotes years and years to ministry
Ministry gains international status
Millions of lives touched all around the world

One un-dealt with vice
One poor decision
Then another
And another
And others

Then suddenly – Exposure!

Everything shakes that can be shaken
Shock, disappointment, surprise, despair
The crowds yell, "Crucify him!"
The church worldwide is vilified
"Hypocrites!" "Fakes!" "Liars!"
The truth and essence of Christianity is attacked

Saints waver
Some slip
Some fall
Some turn away

When the dust settles
In spite of it all
Jesus is still the way, the truth and the life

So don't get distracted
Keep your eyes on Him
He is the author and finisher of your faith
Trust in Him
Not in man
For God alone is perfect
Flesh shall fail.

Remember to pray for our pastors and leaders in the Body of Christ.
They need our prayers.
Selah!

*Scripture*    *Brethren, pray for us.* (1 Thessalonians 5:25 NKJV)

# Day 21

## THINGS ARE DIFFERENT...WHAT HAPPENED?

Remember when you used to spend regular time with God, Remember when you would set aside a part of each day to seek His face and be in His presence even if in the wee hours of the morning, Remember when you prayed to Him because you valued and enjoyed Him and not just because you needed something from Him, Remember when He was more to you than a crisis manager, a need supplier, when you had more than a "I'll pull You out of the closet when I need You and shove You back in when I don't" relationship with Him...
Things are different...What happened?

Remember when you really saw God as a God who is holy and expected you to be holy and live your life as He declared and not just any way you please, Remember when you had reverential respect for His Presence, His House, His Word and His people and never treated any of those things lightly or as common, Remember when it mattered whether your actions and words brought reproach or glory to His Name so you were careful in your behavior and speech, Remember when the thought of giving an account to Him for the deeds done in your life was once a sobering reality for you that influenced your decision-making...
Things are different...What happened?

Remember when you read His Word because you wanted to get to know Him better, because you wanted to learn about Him and His Kingdom and did not see this as a chore, Remember when you read His Word because you knew it was life and food to your spirit and without it you could not survive, Remember when you esteemed His Word as the final authority on moral and ethical issues in your life and not the word of family, friends, government, society or even yourself,

Remember when instead of being uncomfortable, angry and offended, you eagerly welcomed the Truth of His Word and it's ability to teach, correct, reprove, and instruct you in righteousness...
Things are different...What happened?

Remember when you saw it as a privilege and not an obligation to get together with other saints and gather in His Name, Remember when it was a joy to sing praises to Him and to worship Him freely in spirit and in truth no matter who was around, Remember when you felt honored to tell others that you had a personal relationship with Him, that He was a part of your inner circle and not hide it with embarrassment and shame, Remember when He mattered so much to you that you sought to make Him the hub, the central part of every area of your life...
Things are different...What happened?

*Scripture*   Let us examine our ways and test them, and let us return to the Lord.     (Lamentations 3:40 NIV)

# Day 22

## I NEED GOD

..........................................

I need God.

I need Him in every aspect of my life.

I need God.

By the world's standards I am competent in many ways, but apart from Him, I know I can do nothing.

I need God.

I am blessed in innumerable ways, but they all pale in comparison to His presence in my life.

I need God.

I consider it an unfathomable necessity and privilege to be connected to Him.

I need God.

I need Him like the air I breathe.

**I need God.**

Father I unashamedly declare my need for You.

You are my Foundation.

You are my Source.

You are my Reason.

You are my Life.

You are my All.

*Scripture*   Blessed [spiritually prosperous, happy, to be admired] are the poor in spirit [those devoid of spiritual arrogance, those who regard themselves as insignificant], for theirs is the kingdom of heaven [both now and forever].  (Matthew 5:3 AMP)

## Day 23
### WHAT MESSAGE ARE YOU GIVING TO THOSE YOU WORK WITH?

What you laugh at,
What you look at,
What you allow others to show you,
Says a lot to others about you.

About your character,
About your morals,
About your standards,
About how seriously you take your relationship with Christ.

If someone you work with is comfortable sending you, a known Believer, raunchy email,

If someone you work with is comfortable telling you, a known Believer, dirty jokes,

If someone you work with is comfortable showing you, a known Believer, pornographic images, you need to ask yourself why.

Why are they comfortable doing this?
What messages have I given to them directly or indirectly through my conversations and/or my behavior to make them think that doing this is okay?
Where have I dropped the ball in this regard?

What you laugh at,
What you look at,
What you allow others to show you,
Says a lot to others about you.

About your character,
About your morals,
About your standards,
About how seriously you take your relationship with Christ.

Man of God...Woman of God,
What message are you giving to those you work with?

Remember, we are called to be atmospheric changers, not to let our atmospheres change us.

*Scripture* — *You are the light of the world. A city set on a hill cannot be hidden. Nor do men light a lamp and put it under a peck measure, but on a lampstand, and it gives light to all in the house. Let your light so shine before men that they may see your moral excellence and your praiseworthy, noble, and good deeds and recognize and honor and praise and glorify your Father Who is in heaven.* (Matthew 5:14-16 AMPC)

## Day 24
### BUSINESS OR BUSYNESS?

........................................

Business?
or
Busyness?
Which one are you about?

Jesus said He had to be about His Father's business.
He did not say He had to be about His Father's busyness.

Business?
or
Busyness?
Which one are you about?

Busyness is about being busy.
It may or may not be related to business.
All too often people mistakenly equate busyness to business.

Business?
or
Busyness?
Which one are you about?

When it comes to Kingdom work, it's important to have a clear distinction between busy-ness, i.e., doing stuff
and business, i.e., doing what God sanctions and that is producing what is of value and importance to Him.

Selah!

*Scripture*   And He said to them, "Why did you seek Me? Did you not know that I must be about My Father's business?"   (Luke 2:49 NKJV)

# Day 25
## WHAT IS MORE IMPORTANT TO YOU?

**What is more important to you...**
to Please God or to please man?
**What is more important to you...**
to be Esteemed by God or to be esteemed by man?

**What is more important to you...**
the Favor of God or the favor of man?
**What is more important to you...**
Acceptance by God or acceptance by man?

**What is more important to you...**
the Plans of God or the plans of man?
**What is more important to you...**
the Promises of God or the promises of man?

**What is more important to you...**
the Position of God on a matter or the position of man on a matter?
**What is more important to you...**
the Truth of God or the philosophies of man?

**What is more important to you...**
the Word of God or the word of man?
**What is more important to you...**
God's Way or man's way?

**What is more important to you...**
God's Standard or man's standard?
**What is more important to you...**
the Government of God or the government of man?

**What is more important to you...**
Obedience to God or obedience to man?
**What is more important to you...**
to Fear God or to fear man?

**What is more important to you...**
the Judgment of God or the judgment of man?
**What is more important to you...**
God or man?

*Scripture*   Thou shalt have no other gods before me. (Exodus 20:3)

# Day 26

## *I'M A KEPT WOMAN*

............................................

*I*'m a kept woman.
I'm deeply in love and involved with someone who is not my husband and I am unashamedly proud of it.

Why?

Because...

He loves me so much it blows my mind...
He knows everything about me, the good, the bad, and the ugly, yet still wants to be with me... He cares about every aspect of my life and well-being...
He is patient, kind, gentle, strong, forgiving, merciful and gracious... He defends and protects me and doesn't like people trying to harm or mess with me...
He's a warrior and fears nothing or no one...
He covers me and makes me feel safe and secure...
He never wants me to worry about anything...
He takes care of me whenever I get sick and helps me get well...
He encourages me and lifts my spirits when I'm down...
He knows everything I need and makes sure I have it, and often gives me gifts just because...
He is wise and readily gives me sound advice no matter the situation...
He lovingly corrects me when I'm wrong and alerts me to danger ahead of time...
He has excellent morals and standards and never violates them...
His character is impeccable...
He is totally reliable and dependable and never disappoints or let's me down...

He never lies or tries to deceive me...
He honors our relationship and is faithful and committed to it...
He loves when we spend uninterrupted time together alone and wants to do it regularly...
He loves when I talk openly about everything and can handle anything I say...
He is always there for me 24/7 and promised never to walk out on me...
He fills me with unspeakable joy...
Most of all, He suffered and died for me and came back to life so we can be together forever...
He is indescribably, unquestionably, amazing...

The way He keeps me, I'd be a fool to leave Him.

Selah!

*Scripture*  Because your love is better than life, my lips will glorify you.
(Psalm 63:3 NIV)

# Day 27

## FUTURE WORRIES?

............................................

Why do you worry about your future?
Why do you wonder how you are going to make it?

Have you lost sight of who I AM?
Am I not God?
Did I not step out on nothingness, speak into nothingness and create all things?
Can any circumstance be larger than My potential?

Why do you worry about your future?
Why do you wonder how you're going to make it?

Am I not your Father?
Do I not love you?
Do you think I sent my Son to die for you then just leave you helpless?
Has there ever been a time when I did not meet your needs?

Why do you worry about your future?
Why do you wonder how you're going to make it?

Do I not take care of the flowers, grass, and birds that mean far less to Me?
Do you not understand that everything in this earth realm belongs to Me, it is all Mine?
Have I ever neglected you in the past?
Is the future not in My hands?

Why do you worry about your future?
Why do you wonder how you're going to make it?

Still your mind and have faith in Me.
Still your emotions and trust in Me.
Position yourself to hear then obey Me.
Seek first My Kingdom and righteousness and I will add to your life all that you need.

Why do you worry about your future?
Why do you wonder how you're going to make it?

SELAH!

*Scripture*   *I am the Lord, the God of all mankind. Is anything too hard for me?*
(Jeremiah 32:27 NIV)
(Also read Matthew 6:25-34)

# Day 28

## THE BLOOD IS CRYING OUT

If you listen in the spirit you will hear a sound,
The blood of our young men is crying from the ground,
Fatally wounded by wielded guns and knives,
What a senseless horror, what a tragic loss of lives.

Busting out your house like a runner in a race,
One thing in your heart, a life to be erased,
You're all out of order and you're way overboard,
Cause in The Book it's written that vengeance is the Lord's.

Young men wake up the devil has you blind,
He's playing your emotions and messing with your minds,
He's telling you you're all that by taking someone out,
He's dishing you the lie that violence gives you clout.

But there's a Day coming that we'll all have to face,
No matter what our age, creed, color, or race,
The blood will cry out louder and all shall come to light,
Whatcha gonna do then with all your so-called might?

If you listen in the spirit you will hear a sound,
The blood of our young men is crying from the ground,
Murder in our nation is unquestionably off the chart,
Don't sit, blame and point fingers, but find and do your part.

**SELAH!**

*Scriptures*  And Cain said to his brother, Let us go out to the field. And when they were in the field, Cain rose up against Abel his brother and killed him. And the Lord said to Cain, Where is Abel your brother? And he said, I do not know. Am I my brother's keeper? And [the Lord] said, What have you done? The voice of your brother's blood is crying to Me from the ground. And now you are cursed by reason of the earth, which has opened its mouth to receive your brother's [shed] blood from your hand.
(Genesis 4:8-11 AMPC)

*You shall not commit murder.* (Exodus 20:13 AMPC)

# Day 29
## A DIFFERENT KIND OF THANKS...

I thank God for my experience of being sick because it was through sickness that I got to know Him as Jehovah Rapha, my Healer.

I thank Him for encountering times of need because it was in those times that I got to know Him as Jehovah Jireh, my Provider.

I thank Him for seasons of loneliness and unconnectedness because it was in those "empty places", I got to know Him as Jehovah Shamma, the Lord who is present, the One who is always here.

I thank Him for the times the enemy rose against me through people and situations for that is how I got to see Him fight on my behalf and know Him as Jehovah Sabboath, the Lord of Hosts.

I thank Him for the people who did me wrong and upon whom I sought no revenge because their actions and my response allowed me to know Him as Jehovah Gmolah, the God of recompense, the One who repays.

I thank Him for encountering confusion, stress, turmoil and unrest because it was in those times that I got to know Him as Jehovah Shalom, my Peace.

I thank Him for the situations where people in high places set out to disadvantage me but He intervened in my favor showing who really rules and carries the clout, allowing me to know Him as El Elyon, the Most High God.

I thank Him for keeping me from going certain places I wanted to go and doing certain things I wanted to do because it enabled me to know Him as Jehovah Maccaddeshem, the Lord who sanctifies and sets apart.

I thank Him for the times I've failed Him and fallen into sin, exposing my inadequacies and my inability to do right in my own strength, because it allowed me to know Him as Jehovah Tsidkenu, my Righteousness.

I thank Him for the times when I was lost and needed direction and spiritual insight because it caused me to look to His leading and get to know Him as Jehovah Rohi, my Shepherd.

I thank Him for the "close scrapes" in my life because it was through them that I got to know Him as Jehovah, Nissi, my Banner that covers me, keeps me and preserves my life.

I thank God for every mountain He's helped me over and for every test, trial and hardship that He's seen me through.

*Scripture*  *Rejoice always, pray continually, give thanks in all circumstances; for this is God's will for you in Christ Jesus.*
(1 Thessalonians 5:16-18 NIV)

# Day 30

## A THOUGHT ABOUT TRUST

·······················································

If you can trust God with the salvation of your soul,
you can trust Him to provide our daily needs.

If you can trust God with your eternal destination,
you can trust Him to help you overcome any challenges you encounter in life on the way there.

**SELAH!**

*Scripture*  As you go through life, by God's grace, may your position of faith confidently be: "But as for me, I trust in You, O LORD; I say, "You are my God." My times are in Your hand.

(Psalm 31:14-15 NKJV)

# Day 31

## A MESSAGE FROM A GIRL ON THE STREET

...........................................

Because I don't look like you, smell like you, walk like you, talk like you,
Run with you, hang with you, eat with you, bang with you,
Dress like you, sit like you, impress like you, fit like you,
You scorn and you judge and you look down on me,
But there's more, so much more than your eyes can see.

We've not been dealt the same hand in life,
Yours is smooth, mine is rough filled with misery and strife,
Your parents you knew, mine I only knew of,
What you needed was there, mine trickled in with no love.
You scorn and you judge and you look down on me,
But there's more, so much more than your eyes can see.

Look closer and you'll see purpose encased in my mess,
A glimmer of hope radiating through all of my stress,
Like a butterfly from a cocoon one day I'll be free,
And fly gracefully to the flower of my destiny.
You scorn and you judge and you look down on me,
But there's more, so much more than your eyes can see.

There's so much more than your eyes can see.

### Look!

*Scripture*  Do not judge and criticize and condemn others, so that you may not be judged and criticized and condemned yourselves. For just as you judge and criticize and condemn others, you will be judged and criticized and condemned, and in accordance with the measure you [use to] deal out to others, it will be dealt out again to you.  (Matthew 7:1-2 AMPC)

# Day 32

## THE PATH TO PURPOSE

The path to purpose is not a straight line…it has twists, turns, highs and lows,
The path to purpose is not a walk in the park…it will take you places you may not want to go.

The path to purpose is not as easy as pie…it requires death to self, some hardship and tears,
The path to purpose is not achieved overnight…it often takes years and years.

The path to purpose is not always clear…sometimes it is shrouded and grey,
The path to purpose is not always dear…at times you want to walk away.

The path to purpose doesn't always make sense…it will cause you to be misunderstood,
The path to purpose will at times be tense…but it's all working out for your good.

The path to purpose to the eye of the flesh…may seem meaningless and without reward,
The path to purpose to the eye of the spirit…has joy and great riches in God.

The path to purpose often lacks support…you may walk alone and in scorn,
The path to purpose may not be illustrious…but it's indeed where greatness in born.

The path to purpose is not your choice...it's a predestined part of God's plan,
The path to purpose leads to true life...so embrace it by God's grace you can.

*Scriptures* *"For I know the plans I have for you," declares the Lord, "plans to prosper you and not to harm you, plans to give you hope and a future."* (Jeremiah 29:11 NIV)

*For we are God's handiwork, created in Christ Jesus to do good works, which God prepared in advance for us to do.* (Ephesians 2:10 NIV)

## Day 33

### FIX YOUR GAZE UPON ME

..........................................

Listen my child.

I love you.
I care for you.
I care about every detail of your life.

I know things are not where you want them to be.
I know things are not moving as quickly as you want them to move.
I know you are perplexed.

Listen my child.
No, no...don't say anything...Sssshhhhh...listen.
Take your eyes off of your circumstances and gaze upon me.

Gaze upon Me.

Fix your focus on Me.
Lay aside your wants, your needs, your desires, your dreams, your wishes, your concerns, and fix your gaze upon Me.

Look at Me.
Really look at Me.
For as you fix your gaze upon Me, you will discover that I am really all you need.

Do you not realize that in Me lies the fulfillment of your deepest wants, needs, desires, dreams, and wishes?
That in Me lies the answers to your perplexing situations,
That in Me lies the keys to the doors of your future,
That in Me lies perfect peace.

It's all in Me.

So look away from your circumstances my child.
Look away and fix your gaze upon Me.
For it is in Me that you will find it all.

Fix your gaze upon Me.

*Scripture*  *You will keep him in perfect peace, whose mind is stayed on You, Because he trusts in You.*          (Isaiah 26:3 NKJV)

# Day 34

## TO THE BATTLE WEARY

••••••••••••••••••••••••••••••••••••

To those who have tried, denied, submitted, served, changed, bent over backwards,

To those who have listened, counseled, encouraged, exhorted, warned, advised, instructed,

To those who have given, sacrificed, sustained, upheld, remained, stood by, trusted,

To those who have fasted, prayed, believed, decreed, declared, hoped, expected,

To those who have done all these things and seen little or no results and feel like they no longer have the strength, the fortitude, or even the will to continue,

Hold on, your change is coming.

*Scripture* But those who wait for the Lord [who expect, look for, and hope in Him] shall change and renew their strength and power; they shall lift their wings and mount up [close to God] as eagles [mount up to the sun]; they shall run and not be weary, they shall walk and not faint or become tired.     (Isaiah 40:31 AMPC)

## Day 35

### GOOD MORNING...WHAT A BEAUTIFUL DAY!

..................................................

A larm clock rings...
eyes open...
cloudless blue sky...
warm golden sunshine...
cool gentle breeze...
melodious birds...
green leaves dancing...
awareness of Your presence...
good morning - what a beautiful day!

*Scripture*  This is the day the Lord has made; We will rejoice and be glad in it. (Psalm 118:24 NKJV)

# Day 36

## SOMEONE'S STANDING IN THE GAP FOR YOU

You're going through a difficult situation.
People are around you but not with you.

They're physically present, but not attuned to the frequency of your pain.
They have no idea what's going on inside of you.

They have no idea of the hurt, the anxiety, the fear, the disappointment,
the threatening dark cloud of depression.

They see you smile and carry out your daily responsibilities as usual.
They think you're fine and you glibly play along with their perception.

Because of their lack of insight into your real state, you feel all alone.
You wonder if anyone cares.
You wonder if anyone remembers you in their prayers.

Today I say to you, take heart.
Today I say to you, don't despair.

You may feel alone, but you're not alone for God is with you.
He promised to never leave you nor forsake you.
Even though you may not sense His presence, know that He is there.

Know too that although you may not know who,
He's laid you on someone's heart.
He's stirred up their spirit to intercede on your behalf.
They're crying out your name and lifting you up before Him.

They're standing in the gap for you.

So be encouraged.

Take heart.

Someone's standing in the gap for you.

*Scripture* *Pray at all times (on every occasion, in every season) in the Spirit, with all [manner of] prayer and entreaty. To that end keep alert and watch with strong purpose and perseverance, interceding in behalf of all the saints (God's consecrated people).*

(Ephesians 6:18 AMPC)

# Day 37

## FOR ALL THE "MIS" PEOPLE

Misconceived
Misshapen
Misfit
Mistreated
Misheard
Misunderstood
Misquoted
Misrepresented
Misconstrued
Misled
Mishandled
Mistrusted
Misguided
Misplaced

Misfortune?
Mishap?
Mistake?

Mission!

Selah!

*Scripture* *All praise to God, the Father of our Lord Jesus Christ. God is our merciful Father and the source of all comfort. He comforts us in all our troubles so that we can comfort others. When they are troubled, we will be able to give them the same comfort God has given us.*
(2 Corinthians 1:3-4 NLT)

# Day 38

## TRANSITIONING AGAIN

...............................................

A Word
a mandate
shifting gears

transitioning again
overwhelm threatens
questions arise

remembering the Word
trusting Him
receiving His peace

following His lead
moving ahead
resting in Him

*Scriptures* Have I not commanded you? Be strong and courageous. Do not be afraid; do not be discouraged, for the Lord your God will be with you wherever you go. (Joshua 1:9 NIV)

For I know the plans I have for you," declares the Lord, "plans to prosper you and not to harm you, plans to give you hope and a future. (Jeremiah 29:11 NIV)

# Day 39

## ENCOURAGEMENT FOR FRUSTRATED WIVES

..............................................

As priest of the home
why doesn't he pray?
When the kids want his company
why doesn't he stay?

I know we need money
to live and survive,
But if he's working all the time
our family can't thrive.

I remember the times
we used to go out on dates,
But now all he does
Is come home tired and late.

He hardly gives affection
but is always ready for sex,
That's not easy at all
it really makes me vexed.

When I try to talk
I'm seen as a nag,
But if I sit and say nothing
things will continue to sag.

I ask him to help
with things around the house,
He simply refuses
I can't believe my spouse!

When he gets very angry
he screams and shouts,
He curses and threatens to hit me
I'm too ashamed to let that out.

I still go to church
in spite of my plight,
I sing, clap and praise
and try to do what is right.

Oh God I'm so lonely
I feel tied and bound,
My face has a smile
but my spirit is so down.

Now I've met another man
who says he'd be my all,
He is so caring and tempting
Lord I don't want to fall!

Lord this is so hard
I need a breakthrough,
There's no where to turn
so I'm clinging to you.

My sister, my sister
you're tired and worn,
You're bleeding inside
but all hope is not gone.

God knows your desires
He knows your heart,
He feels the pain
that's tearing you apart.

He hears your longing
He hears your cry,
He hears your questions
"Lord how long? Lord Why?"

Things may seem bleak now
you weep and you mourn,
But after your midnight
there will be dawn.

*Scripture*   *No test or temptation that comes your way is beyond the course of what others have had to face. All you need to remember is that God will never let you down; he'll never let you be pushed past your limit; he'll always be there to help you come through it.*
(1 Corinthians 10:13 MSG)

## Day 40
### I AM SOVEREIGN

*I* have a plan, a sovereign plan,
that will not be changed by any man,
Come with whatever and do what you may,
this plan is in place and it will stay.

Yes you have power and authority,
but do not forget that it comes from Me,
Because I have given you some influence and say,
it does not mean you will have it your way.

Remember my child at the core of it all,
I am the One who makes the last call,
So please keep this in mind and know your place,
it will save you much hassle as you run the race.

Selah!

*Scriptures* Who is he who speaks and it comes to pass, if the Lord has not authorized and commanded it? (Lamentations 3:37 AMPC)

*From eternity to eternity I am the only God, says the Lord. No one can oppose what I do. No one can reverse my actions.*
(Isaiah 43:13 NLT)

# Day 41
## TONIGHT I THANK GOD

Tonight I thank God for health...
I know what it is to be sick.
Tonight I thank God for peace...
I know what it is to have inner turmoil.

Tonight I thank God for joy...
I know what it is to feel sorrow.
Tonight I thank God for wisdom...
I know what it is to not know what to do.

Tonight I thank God for provision...
I know what it is to not know how certain needs would be met.
Tonight I thank God for second chances...
I know what it is to mess up real bad.

Tonight I thank God for protection...
I know what it is to face danger.
Tonight I thank God for strength...
I know what it is to be weak.

Tonight I thank God for acceptance...
I know what it is to be rejected.
Tonight I thank God for hope...
I know what it is to despair.

Tonight I thank God for faith...
I know what it is to doubt.
Tonight I thank God for forgiveness...
I know what it is to stand condemned.

Tonight I thank God for His abiding presence...
I know what it is to feel lonely.
Tonight I thank God for mountains...
I know what it is to be in the valley.

Tonight I thank God for being His child...
I know what it is to not be a part of His family.

**TONIGHT I THANK GOD.**

*Scripture* Oh, give thanks to the Lord, for He is good! For His mercy endures forever. (Psalms 107:1 NKJV)

# Day 42
## DON'T

....................................................

*D*on't.

Don't put a comma where God wants a full stop.

Don't give up the 80% you have in your spouse for the 20% you see in someone else.

Don't compare yourself with others.

Don't build your life on someone else's dream.

Don't measure your success by someone else's yardstick.

Don't try to be who you're not.

Don't compromise your standards just to fit in.

Don't forget you can't change people.

Don't look to another person to do or be what only God can do or be.

Don't forget Jesus is coming again.

Don't.

*Scripture*   Let the one who is wise heed these things and ponder the loving deeds of the Lord.          (Psalms 107:43 NIV)

# Day 43
## *TRUST HIM WHEN YOU CAN'T TRACE HIM*

Fasting
Praying
Seeking
Longing
Waiting
Crying
Praising
Worshipping

No answer
No instruction
No intervention
No revelation
No understanding
No comfort
No presence
No anything

"GOD WHAT IS GOING ON…WHERE ARE YOU???"

Wait…Listen

He's there…Right there

He sees
He knows
He understands
He loves
He cares
He's at work

## TRUST HIM WHEN YOU CAN'T TRACE HIM!

*Scripture*   *And lo, I am with you always [remaining with you perpetually—regardless of circumstance, and on every occasion], even to the end of the age.*                              (Matthew 28:20 AMP)

# Day 44

## WHEN YOU GO INTO WORK TODAY

...........................................

When you go into work today...
See things from God's view,
Know the Holy Spirit is with you to help you,
Remember God is on your side.

When you go into work today...
Have an attitude of gratitude,
Let the joy of the Lord be your strength,
Let His peace within radiate without.

When you go into work today...
Work as unto the Lord,
Walk in honesty and integrity,
Decide to walk in love.

When you go into work today...
Speak life and not death into the atmosphere,
Respect your coworkers no matter their position,
Honor your relationship with your spouse.

When you go into work today...
Know you are salt and light,
Be on alert for Kingdom assignments,
Remember you represent Christ.

*Scripture*  Let your light so shine before men, that they may see your good works, and glorify your Father which is in heaven.

(Matthew 5:16)

## BE STILL

...........................................

*B*e still.

Be still and know that I am God.

I will be exalted in your situation.

Rest in Me.

Take refuge in Me.

Be still and know that I am God.

Be still.

Quiet your self before Me and be still.

Allow me to cleanse you, be still.

Put your mind on the altar and be still.

Be still and know, absolutely know, beyond a shadow of a doubt know, that I am God.

I've got this.

Be still.

Be still.
Be still.

*Scripture*   *Be still, and know that I am God; I will be exalted among the nations, I will be exalted in the earth!*   (Psalms 46:10 NKJV)

# Day 46

## WHO ARE YOU BEHIND CLOSED DOORS?

........................................

Who are you behind closed doors...
when away from the people to whom you are accountable in your life?

Who are you behind closed doors...
when away from your husband?
when away from your wife?

Who are you behind closed doors...
when away from your family?
when away from your godly friends?

Who are you behind closed doors...
when away from your pastor and the leaders of your place of worship?
when away from your brothers and sisters in Christ?

Who are you behind closed doors...
when away from your boss?
when away from your business partners?

Who are you behind closed doors...
when away from the citizens of your country in a foreign land?
when absolutely no one else is around?

**Who are you behind closed doors?**

Is the person you are behind closed doors starkly different from the person you are in the open?

Is your "private life" at odds with your "public life"?

If so, it's time to close the gap and make it right before the Lord.

### Who are you behind closed doors?

It matters to God and should therefore matter to you.

Selah!

*Scripture*  For God will bring every deed into judgment, including every hidden thing, whether it is good or evil.

(Ecclesiastes 12:14 NLT)

# Day 47

## THERE'S A PLACE IN YOUR HEART

............................................

There's a place in your heart
That's for God and God alone,

There's a place in your heart
Where He's established His throne,

There's a place in your heart
You need to beware,

Trouble will come if another sits there.

*Scripture*  For thou shalt worship no other god: for the Lord, whose name is Jealous, is a jealous God.  (Exodus 34:14)

## Day 48
### HOW TO RUN ON "E"

........................................

TRY TO DO
Everything
For
Everyone, Everytime, Everywhere
at your Expense
and
God's
Exclusion

and

TRY TO BE
Everything
To
Everyone, Everytime, Everywhere
at your Expense
and
God's
Exclusion

and

YOU WILL END UP RUNNING ON
"E"
EMPTY!

Selah!

*Scriptures* *Ignorant zeal is worthless; haste makes waste.*
*(Proverbs 19:2 MSG)*

*Trust God from the bottom of your heart; don't try to figure out everything on your own. Listen for God's voice in everything you do, everywhere you go; he's the one who will keep you on track. Don't assume that you know it all. Run to God! Run from evil!*
(Proverbs 3:5-7 MSG)

## Day 49
### REJECTION...A GIFT?

..........................................

Situation

Rejection

Hurt

Pain

Isolation

Presence

Communion

Comfort

Clarity

Strength

Growth

Gratitude

Praise

It is often through rejection that we experience isolation, and through isolation that we better hear the voice of God and have the opportunity to experience clarity, instruction, and exponential growth, making what we thought to be an enemy, a gift in disguise.

Selah!

*Scripture*   For we do not have a High Priest who is unable to sympathize and understand our weaknesses and temptations, but One who has been tempted [knowing exactly how it feels to be human] in every respect as we are, yet without [committing any] sin. Therefore let us [with privilege] approach the throne of grace [that is, the throne of God's gracious favor] with confidence and without fear, so that we may receive mercy [for our failures] and find [His amazing] grace to help in time of need [an appropriate blessing, coming just at the right moment].

(Hebrews 4:15-16 AMP)

# Day 50
## COME APART

••••••••••••••••••••••••••••••••••••••••

Come apart

Or

Come apart

Selah!

*Scripture*    Come to Me, all you who labor and are heavy-laden and overburdened, and I will cause you to rest. [I will ease and relieve and refresh your souls.] Take My yoke upon you and learn of Me, for I am gentle (meek) and humble (lowly) in heart, and you will find rest (relief and ease and refreshment and recreation and blessed quiet) for your souls.       (Matthew 11:28-29 AMPC)

# Day 51

## DON'T DESPAIR...HOPE

............................................

**H**ave to focus on God and His Word

n**O**thing or no one else can see me through

resting in this dwelling **P**lace

H**E**'s more than enough

*Scripture*   *My soul, wait only upon God and silently submit to Him; for my hope and expectation are from Him.*     (Psalms 62:5 AMPC)

## Day 52

## ABORTION???...AN UNBORN CHILD'S PLEA

........................................................

Hi mommy it's me the one you've conceived,
I know right now my presence brings you grief,
You did not expect me at this point in your life,
It messes with your plans and cuts like a knife.
But please mommy, please hear my plea,
Please give me a chance, please don't abort me.

I may not have come the way that you wanted,
That one act of sex leaves your mind haunted,
My daddy has left, disowning you and me,
You're broken, you're hurt and racked with misery.
But please mommy, please hear my plea,
Please give me a chance, please don't abort me.

Mommy guess what, I am really alive,
I'm not a cluster of cells, but a real soul inside,
I'm filled with potential, talent, and ability,
There's much I want to do for you, others, and me.
So please mommy, please hear my plea,
Please give me a chance, please don't abort me.

I see you holding and rocking me while I gaze in your eyes,
I see me giving you big hugs and kisses because you're my prize,
I want to skip, I want to dance, I want to play and sing,
I want to learn and help others and live out my destiny.
So please mommy, please hear my plea,
Please give me a chance, please don't abort me.

Can you step back a moment from your turmoil and strife?
Can you consider that in the balance you hold my life?
Ask God for His help to keep me, and you,
I believe if you trust Him He'll see us through.
So please mommy, please hear my plea,
Please give me a chance, please don't abort me.

Mommy if by some chance you feel I'm too much,
To guilt and condemnation please do not clutch,
I prefer you to raise me but I'll understand,
If you think it's best to place me in someone else's loving hands.
So please mommy, please, please hear my plea,
Please give me a chance, please don't kill me.

Selah!

*Scripture*  *For you created my inmost being; you knit me together in my mother's womb. I praise you because I am fearfully and wonderfully made; your works are wonderful, I know that full well.*  (Psalm 139:13-14 NIV)

# Day 53

## FOR THOSE GOING THROUGH

•••••••••••••••••••••••••••••••••••••••••••••

For those going through,
Through times of struggle and uncertainty,
Through times of depression and despair,
Through times of confusion and perplexity…

For those going through,
Through times of pain and disappointment,
Through times of turmoil and distress,
Through times of fear and doubt…

For those going through,
Through times of sickness and dis-ease,
Through times of discouragement and apathy,
Through times of existing and not living…

For those going through,
Through times when prayers seem to hit the ceiling and bounce back,
Through times when a praise is a push instead of a pleasure,
Through times when faith is faltering and fading…

For those going through,
Know that this too shall pass,
God is at work,
And He's turning your situation around for you.

Keep standing, keep hoping, keep trusting, keep believing, keep praying,
for at the appointed time, your change will come.

*Scripture*  Weeping may endure for a night, But joy comes in the morning.
(Psalms 30:5 NKJV)

# Day 54
## BEWARE OF SCORN

If you have a strong, fit and healthy body,
Beware not to scorn others who don't.

If you hold a position of leadership and authority in some area,
Beware not to scorn others who don't.

If you have a well-paying job with a position of influence and power,
Beware not to scorn others who don't.

If you are smart and catch on to things quickly,
Beware not to scorn others who don't.

If you have a successful and profitable business,
Beware not to scorn others who don't.

If you have a marriage that is happy and fulfilling,
Beware not to scorn others who don't.

If you have focused, well-behaved children that do not give you problems,
Beware not to scorn others who don't.

If you have a close-knit loving family who will stand by you through any situation,
Beware not to scorn others who don't.

If you have money over and above to meet your needs,
Beware not to scorn others who don't.

If you have shoes and clothes that are fashionable and costly,
Beware not to scorn others who don't.

If you live in a nice house or neighborhood,
Beware not to scorn others who don't.

If you drive a nice vehicle,
Beware not to scorn others who don't.

If you have gifts, talents and abilities that help you excel in particular areas,
Beware not to scorn others who don't.

If you have a ministry that is effective and expanding,
Beware not to scorn others who don't.

If you have a relationship with God through Jesus Christ,
Beware not to scorn others who don't.

If you have a mature relationship with God and a good understanding of His Kingdom,
Beware not to scorn others who don't.

Beware not to scorn others who are, or who you think are in some way less fortunate than you.

Remember, every good thing that you have or experience is because of the goodness, grace and blessing of God on your life.

Remember also that you have not finished living yet and do not know what your future holds.

Selah!

*Scriptures* *Pride goes before destruction, and a haughty spirit before a fall.*
*(Proverbs 16:18 NKJV)*

*Surely He scorns the scornful, but gives grace to the humble.*
*(Proverbs 3:34 NKJV)*

# Day 55

## GOD SEES AND GOD KNOWS

..........................................

Lord,
This is hard.
This is so, so, hard.

I don't think I can handle this?
Why aren't You changing this situation?

The questions run deep.
They swirl around my mind like a whirlwind, tumbling over all that was once so settled, so stable, so secure, so planned.

Do You not see what is happening to me?
Do You not know what I am dealing with?

Lord, do You see?
Lord, do You know?

I see.
I know.
Trust Me.

*Scripture*   Fear not, for I have redeemed you; I have called you by your name; You are Mine. When you pass through the waters, I will be with you; And through the rivers, they shall not overflow you. When you walk through the fire, you shall not be burned, Nor shall the flame scorch you.            (Isaiah 43:1-2 NKJV)

## Day 56
### PERFECT PASTORS

........................................

Do you have an unspoken belief that Pastors should be perfect?

That they should have:

Perfect manners
Perfect deportment
Perfect speech
Perfect dress

Perfect marriages
Perfect spouses
Perfect children
Perfect homes

Perfect people skills
Perfect leadership skills
Perfect communication skills
Perfect decision-making skills

Perfect scriptural knowledge
Perfect scriptural understanding
Perfect scriptural interpretation
Perfect scriptural delivery

Perfect timing
Perfect strength
Perfect availability
Perfect energy
Perfect discernment
Perfect sensitivity
Perfect clarity
Perfect solutions

Perfect administrative know-how
Perfect financial know-how
Perfect marketing know-how
Perfect technological know-how

Perfect faith
Perfect wisdom
Perfect joy
Perfect peace

Perfect emotional habits
Perfect sexual habits
Perfect eating habits
Perfect recreational habits

Do you have an unspoken belief that Pastors should be perfect?

Well if you don't, why do you sometimes act as if you do?

Remember, Pastors, like you, are human too.

Selah!

*Scripture*    Pattern yourselves after me [follow my example], as I imitate and follow Christ (the Messiah).      (1 Corinthians 11:1 AMPC)

# Day 57
## BE STILL...AGAIN

––––––––––––––––––––––––––

**B**E STILL AND KNOW
THAT I AM GOD

BE STILL
not busy
not active
not here and there
not mentally and emotionally all over the place
be still...

AND KNOW
not think
not guess
not assume
not reason
know...

THAT I
not you
not your parents
not your spouse
not your children
not your expended family
not your friend
not your boss
not your doctor
not your pastor
not your circumstances
not the government...

I AM GOD
not was
not will be
not may be
am God.

BE STILL AND KNOW
THAT I AM GOD!

*Scripture*  Let be and be still, and know (recognize and understand) that I am God.                    (Psalm 46:10 AMPC)

# Day 58

## EAGLES SHOW A BETTER WAY

........................................

Situation...
physical flapping
mental flapping
emotional flapping
exhaustion

Situation...
spiritual positioning
expectant waiting
wind
soaring above

How are you dealing with your situation?

Selah!

*Scripture*    *Even the youths shall faint and be weary, and the young men shall utterly fall, But those who wait on the Lord shall renew their strength; They shall mount up with wings like eagles, they shall run and not be weary, they shall walk and not faint.*
(Isaiah 40:30-31)

# Day 59

## MORNING HAIKU

••••••••••••••••••••••••••••••••••

Early morning air
fresh, crisp, pure
dew to my soul

*Scripture*   Great is his faithfulness; his mercies begin afresh each morning.
(Lamentations 3:23 NLT)

# Day 60

## THE SIN-SATIONAL POWER OF LUST

........................................

Lust moved from his heart to his head,
Then he played with the thoughts in his mind,
Next he's acted it out in somebody's bed,
To the plan of the enemy blind.

He flirted boldly with the flesh,
He dabbled knowingly in raw sin,
He tasted "sweet" forbidden waters,
And now the claws are in.

He got up and covered his tracks,
He built up an inner defense,
He told himself he'd never go back,
Removed telltale evidence.

He said "self, now you've got to be smart",
He said "self, now you've got to be slick",
He said "self, now you've got to lie from the start",
If anyone suspects you of this.

But what's unseen is a sinister tie,
His soul with hers has become one,
From this fling he thought he'd easily fly,
But it's much harder to get undone.

She wields her power like a sword,
And down he goes again,
She uses him like a toy when bored,
No love, no care, no pain.

She blazes in and out his life,
Like a fiery shooting comet,
His self-control lost at her beck and call,
He returns like a dog to its vomit.

He thinks, what have I done,
I didn't bargain for all of this,
My wife, my kids, my reputation,
It's all now at high risk.

In panic he begs her their "secret" to hide,
She smiles and laughs silently with scorn,
Then calls up her friends in them to "confide"
Now the fire of gossip is born.

They're shocked, stunned, amazed and surprised,
Not that upstanding Christian family man,
Snickering "don't tell anyone" she advised,
But they had another plan.

He keeps acting like all is cool,
He keeps playing the holy game,
He thinks those around him are obliviously fooled,
That's the sad and absurd shame.

For what he does not realize,
From compromising with this wench,
Where once emanated fragrant holiness,
From his life now comes sin's putrid stench.

He once stood spiritually tall,
Now there is much inner distress,
And because of the terror of losing it all
He won't come clean and confess.

His dark draining double life,
Progressively takes its toll,

Just like a razor-sharp carving knife
It cuts away at his soul.

How will his story end?
Many watch from the sidelines to see,
God wants to heal and mend,
But will he seek help to get free?

Will he trust God and tell the truth?
Will he cast aside pride and live?
Will public exposure come from a sleuth?
Will he ask his wife to forgive?

One thing that's certain for sure,
As he chooses to mill about,
God stands lovingly by to restore,
But time is running out.

His grace He now extends,
Like a soft gentle breeze it blows,
But once it lifts and ends,
Swift judgment He'll impose.

This too common scene reminds us,
To carefully guard our hearts,
Don't be like a horse with no blinders,
Stay focused, reign in lust at the start.

Selah!

*Scriptures* *For out of the heart proceed evil thoughts, murders, adulteries, fornications, thefts, false witness, blasphemies.*
(Matthew 15:19 NKJV)

*Beloved, I implore you as aliens and strangers and exiles [in this world] to abstain from the sensual urges (the evil desires, the passions of the flesh, your lower nature) that wage war against the soul.* (I Peter 2:11 AMPC)

*Let marriage be held in honor (esteemed worthy, precious, of great price, and especially dear) in all things. And thus let the marriage bed be undefiled (kept undishonored); for God will judge and punish the unchaste [all guilty of sexual vice] and adulterous.*
(Hebrews 13:4 AMPC)

# Day 61
## GOD LOVES YOU

........................................

*G*od loves you.
God, loves you.
God loves, you.

Receive and rest in His love!

*Scripture* For I am convinced [and continue to be convinced—beyond any doubt] that neither death, nor life, nor angels, nor principalities, nor things present and threatening, nor things to come, nor powers, nor height, nor depth, nor any other created thing, will be able to separate us from the [unlimited] love of God, which is in Christ Jesus our Lord. (Romans 8:38-39 AMP)

# Day 62
## GOD CAN

..............................................

"Can God?"

"God can."

"God can?"

"God can."

"God can??"

"God can!"

"God can."

*Scripture* — Now to Him who is able to do exceedingly abundantly above all that we ask or think, according to the power that works in us, to Him be glory in the church by Christ Jesus to all generations, forever and ever. Amen (Ephesians 3:20-21 NKJV)

# Day 63
## THOTS ARE POWERFUL

........................................

Thoughts are powerful.

Thoughts create perspectives.
Thoughts generate feelings.
Thoughts birth actions.

Pleasant thoughts create pleasant perspectives.
Pleasant thoughts generate pleasant feelings.
Pleasant thoughts birth pleasant actions.

Unpleasant thoughts create unpleasant perspectives.
Unpleasant thoughts generate unpleasant feelings.
Unpleasant thoughts birth unpleasant actions.

Thoughts are powerful.

You may not have the power to change your situation,
But you do have the power to change your thoughts about your situation.

You may not have the power to change that person,
But you do have the power to change your thoughts about that person.

Changed thoughts create changed perspectives.
Changed thoughts generate changed feelings.
Changed thoughts birth changed actions.

Thoughts are powerful.

Selah!

*Scripture*  Summing it all up, friends, I'd say you'll do best by filling your minds and meditating on things true, noble, reputable, authentic, *compelling, gracious—the best, not the worst; the beautiful, not the ugly; things to praise, not things to curse.*

(Philippians 4:8 MSG)

# Day 64

## SEEK ME FOR ME

You say you have sought Me,
But you did not seek Me,
You sought what you thought you could get from Me.

You say you have sought Me,
But you did not seek Me,
You sought to receive from My hand, not to draw closer to My heart.

You did not seek Me in purity of heart,
You did not seek Me in purity of motive,
You did not seek Me out of love and a desire to build a deeper relationship with Me,
You did not seek Me for Me.

This is not the path for you,
Your path is to draw close to My heart,
Your path is to build a deep abiding relationship with Me...
an unshakeable relationship that can withstand anyone and anything,
That is the path for you.

Seek Me for Me,
Delight yourself in Me,
Not in My power and anointing to intervene in your circumstances, but in Me,
Seek Me for Me.

Seek Me for Me...
Spend time with Me,
Bask in My presence,
Seek My face,

Get to know My ways,
Feed on My Word,
Interact with Me from a place of love,
Seek Me for Me.

Seek Me for Me,
Do this in purity of heart,
Do this is in sincerity of motive,
Seek Me for Me.

Seek Me for Me,
Do this, and out of your relationship with Me,
The anointing on your life will increase,
The desires of your heart will be fulfilled,
Seek Me for Me.

SEEK ME FOR ME.

Selah.

*Scriptures* *When You said, "Seek My face [in prayer, require My presence as your greatest need]," my heart said to You, " Your face, O Lord, I will seek [on the authority of Your word].* (Psalm 27:8 AMP)

*Delight yourself in the Lord, And He will give you the desires and petitions of your heart.* (Psalm 37:4 AMP)

# Day 65

## CAN I BE HONEST?

........................................

If I were honest, could you take it?
Or would you subtly try to shake it?

Well watch out, here goes,
This may be some unlikely prose.

I'm tired, yeah, tired;
Saved, sanctified, filled with the Holy Ghost and tired.

Tired of what? You ask.

Do you really want to go there?
Okay, but you'd better beware.

I'm tired of the form and fashion;

I'm tired of the hype without the power;

I'm tired of the bless me, me, me, me, me vibe;

I'm tired of the four steps to over the edge of the cliff, oops, I mean victory......why do we keep trying to put God into a formula or a box, or think we can second guess His every move?

I'm tired of the same old 4 fast songs + 4 slow songs + 3 hallelujahs in between = praise and worship?

I'm tired of the titles without the authority;
I'm tired of the Nicolaitan spirit suppressing the royal priesthood;

I'm tired of the endless, empty, clanging of "Christianese"...What's up with that anyhow?

I'm tired of the pressure to fit into someone's concept of who I am… whatever happened to allowing people to be the unique creation who Christ created them to be?

I'm tired of being invited to walk into a season that seems to evade me with each step I take;

I'm tired of the "required" "churchy clothes", "churchy hairdo's" and the "churchy attitude";

I'm tired of the cookouts, bake sales, banquets, car washes…whatever happened to tithing and giving…does God's way not work anymore? Have we become so selfish that we can no longer give without immediately receiving in return?

I'm tired of the entertainment, the spectatorship, the gotta be a star in "church" because I can't be one in the world syndrome;

I'm tired of effectively hearing the Word, but not effectively doing the Word;

I'm tired of being expected to look the part, act the part, be the part…by the way, what's the part?

I'm tired of going to church instead of being the church;

I'm tired of the empty hugs, the empty greetings, the empty smiles, the lack of genuine love;

I'm tired of the "our ministry is doing this", "our ministry is doing that", "well I heard the ministry down the road is doing"…toot, toot, blow, blow, brag, brag…ouch my head hurts!!

Are the people being saved, healed, delivered, equipped with the Word, and helped to discover and walk in their God-ordained Kingdom purpose and thereby impact the earth as God desires?…Are disciples being made? Hhhhhmmmm.

I'm tired of the debate about the carpet...does it ever dawn on you that we are more interested in worshipping God in spirit and truth so we don't care what color the carpet is, or even if there is carpet?

I'm tired of the "he took my members and left the church" story...How can a pastor say that someone took his or her members when they don't belong to the pastor in the first place?
Was it not Jesus who died on the cross and shed His own blood to purchase us as members of His Body and as His own possession?
And since there is only one church, how can a Believer leave the church unless he/she
renounces his/her faith in Christ?...Hhhhmmmm.

Wrongfully or rightfully, I'm just tired.

Complaining? – No.

A lone voice? – No.

Being honest and saying what many other Believers are afraid to say because of the risk of being misunderstood, criticized, hated or even ostracized – Yes.

I believe I speak for thousands of others of like-spirit scattered across the globe eagerly anticipating a change,

For Lord we simply want to love, relate to, be empowered by, worship, and serve You together in light of Your Word and Your Kingdom purposes.

Now honestly, is that asking too much?

Selah!

*Scripture*  Yet a time is coming and has now come when the true worshipers will worship the Father in the Spirit and in truth, for they are the kind of worshipers the Father seeks. God is spirit, and his worshipers must worship in the Spirit and in truth.

(John 4:23-24 NIV)

# Day 66

## POW-HER

..............................................

POW-HER

IS NOT

POWER

IT IS VIOLENCE!!!

Selah!

*Scripture*  *The Lord tests and proves the [unyieldingly] righteous, but His soul abhors the wicked and him who loves violence.*
*(Psalms 11:5 AMPC)*

# Day 67
## *THIS LIFE ON EARTH CAN BE HARD*

..........................................

This life on earth can be hard.

Just stop a moment.

Stop.

Look around.

Look at the faces that pass your way...

The face of the mother that parents her children alone under the weight of economic hardship...

The face of the teenage boy as he seeks fulfillment through violent, disruptive gang membership...

The face of the prominent doctor as he faces the consequences of unethical behavior...

The face of the successful businessman as he wonders what or who will be the next victim of financial warfare...

The face of the unkempt woman as she goes from car to car begging for money, ignored, despised, rejected...

The face of the tourist enslaved by the desire for monetary fulfillment, driven to the vice-like grip of the world of gambling and ensnared...

The face of the politician as his desire to serve the people of his nation is slain by the dragon of self-greed...

The face of the teacher as she fights to instill the value of education within her students in spite of little moral, social, and financial support...

The face of the criminal as he approaches the gallows, a man dead long ago, strangled by anger and hatred manifested in violence…

The face of the wife confronted by the adulterous dealings of her husband, paralyzed by shock, unbelief, hurt and despair…

The face of the baby in hospital, born with AIDS, born with a reduced chance to live…

The face of the father as his teenage daughter announces her unplanned pregnancy…

The face of the cocaine addict as he scavenges for money, food, or wares to acquire the very thing that has him catapulting down the road to self-destruction…

The face of the Christian who has become entangled in the tentacles of sin, seemingly paralyzed by the enemy of the faith…

The face of the pastor as he looks on these faces and falls on his knees crying out to God for their souls and their healing, deliverance, and salvation…

My face as I glance at it in the mirror while writing these reflections.

Stop.

Look around.

Look at the faces that pass your way.

No doubt.
This life on earth can be hard.

*Scripture*  *These things I have spoken unto you, that in me ye might have peace. In the world ye shall have tribulation: but be of good cheer; I have overcome the world.*  (John 16:33)

# Day 68
## GRACE

........................................

Bad decision
tears fears prayers
floods of refreshing peace

*Scripture*  *If we confess our sins, He is faithful and just to forgive us our sins and to cleanse us from all unrighteousness.*          (I John 1:9)

# Day 69

## TO MOTHERS WITH A WAYWARD CHILD

You look in dismay at your wayward child,
And wonder, how on earth did he/she get so wild,
When from a small babe upon your knee,
You taught and trained him/her Biblically.

You hang your head down in guilt and shame,
You feel like somehow you are to blame,
"Friends" gossip meanly behind your back,
People point their fingers in scornful attack.

Your heart deeply pains and severely aches,
The thoughts in your mind rock you like an earthquake,
You say, Lord Jesus, this is too much stress,
But Woman of God, you have to press.

God sees each one of your many tears,
He hears each one of your many prayers,
He feels the weight of your deepest sighs,
He's touched by the shrill of your anguished cries.

Don't give up Woman of God, keep standing on His Word,
Don't give up Woman of God, know you are heard,
Thank and praise Him in advance for the needed change,
Even though it may feel weird, silly, or strange.

Keep your faith alive and don't yield to doubt,
Believe deep in your soul God is working things out,
He's All-Knowing, All-Powerful, so no matter what you see,
He's more than able to set your child free.

So shake yourself mighty warrior and arise,
Set your face like flint and fix your eyes on the prize,
War in the Spirit and in God's time you'll see,
Through Jesus Christ you'll have the victory.

**Encouraging Scriptures for Mothers**

Nehemiah 8:10
Psalms 46:1
Proverbs 3:5-6
Isaiah 41:10, 54:17
Jeremiah 31:16-17
Matthew 19:26
2 Corinthians 10:3-5
Ephesians 3:20-21
Hebrews 6:12, 11:6
1 John 5:14-15

# Day 70

## WORLD CRISIS ABOUNDS

World crisis abounds
fear panic and worry everywhere
resting hoping and trusting in God

*Scripture*    He says, "Be still, and know that I am God; I will be exalted among the nations, I will be exalted in the earth.

(Psalms 46:10 NIV)

# Day 71

## GOD'S LAW VS. HUMAN LAW

......................................

If God's Law declares something to be wrong,
no human legislation can make it right.

A popular or majority vote means nothing in the eyes of God.

If every human being on this planet votes in favor of an activity or
behavior deemed wrong by God,
and every nation of the earth passes laws to support the same,
in God's eyes, that activity or behavior is still wrong and He will judge it
accordingly.

Be not deceived.
No matter what man declares as right,
if God says it is wrong, it is wrong.

*Scriptures* *All your words are true; all your righteous laws are eternal.*
*(Psalms 119:160 NIV)*

*Long ago I learned from your statutes that you established them
to last forever.* *(Psalms 119:152 NIV)*

# Day 72

## TO MY CHILDREN

........................................

May you grow in your personal relationship with God and treat it as the most precious thing you have on this earth…

May you remember to read, study, meditate on and obey the Word, all the days of your lives…

May you never neglect prayer, praise, time in God's presence, or assembling for worship with other Believers…

May you honor your father and me so that it may go well with you, and you may enjoy long life on the earth…

May you take care of your bodies as the temple of the Holy Spirit, do all you can to keep healthy, fit and strong, and abstain from sexual immorality…

May you have the mind of Christ and exercise good judgment in every situation you face…

May you be the unique individuals that God created you to be and not be ensnared by the bondage of comparing yourselves to others…

May you discover and use all your gifts, talents and abilities to the honor and glory of God and the advancement of His Kingdom…

May you find and fulfill God's divine purpose for your lives no matter what it requires of you, knowing His purposes are good…

May you always seek to do your best in every situation and be contented with the results, knowing that you did your best…

May your desire to try always be stronger than your fear of failure, for God has not given you a spirit of fear and you can do all God-honoring things through Christ who strengthens you...

May you work with diligence and excellence and successfully excel in your chosen careers, becoming leaders to the glory of God...

May you do well financially and govern your money according to Kingdom financial principles, faithfully giving to God, taking care of your families, contributing to God's work, helping others in need, and making wise purchases and investments...

May you walk in Divine Favor, in wisdom beyond your years, and come to know the gift of true friendship...

May you joyfully embrace each stage of your lives and seek to honor God wherever you are, whoever you are with, and in whatever you do...

May you abide under God's divine protection with His warring angels and ministering angels encamped around you...

May you choose God-fearing, compatible spouses who love and respect you and seek your best interests should marriage be a part of your future...

May you faithfully pass God's Truth and the principles and values of God's Kingdom on to the next generation...

May you remember that no matter what you face in life, God is always there for you, He will always love you, and He will never fail you...

May you know that I love you and always will.

*Scripture*  *Lo, children are an heritage of the Lord: and the fruit of the womb is his reward.*             (Psalms 127:3)

## Day 73
### CHALLENGES?...BELIEVE GOD

Challenges with your children?
Challenges with your spouse?
Challenges with your family?
BELIEVE GOD.

Challenges with your friends?
Challenges with your job?
Challenges with your finances?
BELIEVE GOD.

Challenges with your health?
Challenges with your mind?
Challenges with your emotions?
BELIEVE GOD.

Challenges with your ministry?
Challenges with your community?
Challenges with your country?
BELIEVE GOD.

What does His Word say?
What is He speaking in your heart?
What has He spoken through a prophetic word?
BELIEVE GOD.

BELIEVE GOD!
BELIEVE GOD!
BELIEVE GOD!

*Scripture*  Trust in the Lord with all your heart, And lean not on your own understanding; In all your ways acknowledge Him, And He shall direct your paths. (Proverbs 3:5-6 NKJV)

# Day 74
## BACK TO SCHOOL ENCOURAGEMENT FOR STUDENTS AND TEACHERS

**Students be encouraged to:**
Study your work every day
Treat your teachers, administrators, custodial staff and fellow students with respect
Understand and keep foremost in your minds that the main reason you are at school is to learn
Don't hang out with anyone who will pull you away from what you know is right and hinder your success
Encourage your peers to do well and behave well
Never be afraid to ask questions
Take advantage of available extra classes and get involved in at least one extra-curricular activity
Set personal goals, aim high, and stay focused

**Teachers be encouraged to:**
Teach with precision, purpose and passion
Encourage your students to maximize their abilities and soar
Acknowledge and praise all progress no matter how big or small
Choose to be whatever you want to see – your actions will speak louder than any words you may say
Handle "problem students" with firmness, compassion, and care; remember there's a story behind every story
Ensure you know your limits and take mini breaks to de-stress if you feel tempted to explode
Remember you have a strong, potentially life-altering influence on your students so use it well
Support each other when the going gets tough

## Students and Teachers be encouraged to...

*Scripture* *Trust God from the bottom of your heart; don't try to figure out everything on your own. Listen for God's voice in everything you do, everywhere you go; he's the one who will keep you on track. Don't assume that you know it all. Run to God! Run from evil!*
(Proverbs 3:5-7 MSG)

# Day 75

## BUST CAN I TRUST YOU?

........................................

*I* want to endue you with a greater level of power and anointing, but can I trust you?

Can I trust you to speak when I say speak and to be silent when I say to be silent?
Can I trust you to go when I say go and to stay when I say stay?
Can I trust you to give when I say give and to withhold when I say to withhold?

I want to endue you with a greater level of power and anointing, but can I trust you?

Can I trust you to be who I've called you to be and not be like another?
Can I trust you to stand up and resist the pressure of pleasing the crowd and not bow to it?
Can I trust you to speak my pure unadulterated truth and not change it in any way to make it more acceptable?

I want to endue you with a greater level of power and anointing, but can I trust you?

Can I trust you to obey Me above all else and not let your responses to others be based on what they do or do not do, or on your feelings?
Can I trust you to use My methods even though you are mocked and ridiculed and viewed as foolish?
Can I trust you to abstain from that which I tell you to abstain from and not worry about offending another?

I want to endue you with a greater level of power and anointing, but can I trust you?

## Selah!

*Scripture*    For I know the plans and thoughts that I have for you,' says the Lord, 'plans for peace and well-being and not for disaster to give you a future and a hope.            (Jeremiah 29:11 AMP)

# Day 76
## ARE YOU ANCHORED?

........................................

**A**lways
**N**eeding
**C**hrist's
**H**elp
**O**perating
**R**egularly
**E**very
**D**ay

Are you anchored?

*Scriptures* *Trust in and rely confidently on the Lord with all your heart and do not rely on your own insight or understanding. In all your ways know and acknowledge and recognize Him, and He will make your paths straight and smooth [removing obstacles that block your way].* (Proverbs 3:5-6 AMP)

*For in him we live and move and exist.* (Acts 17:28a NLT)

# Day 77

## YOU OR GOD?

..............................................

You expected "A",
God said give "B",
Now I'm treated like a refugee.

You wanted to hear "Yes",
God said to say "No",
Now I have nowhere to go.

You said "come",
God said "stay",
Now I have a price to pay.

You said "move",
God said "wait",
Now you want to separate.

You wanted my help,
God said refrain,
Now you resent the sound of my name.

You wanted me in your box,
God said be free,
This is about Him...not about you nor about me.

### SELAH!

*Scripture*  Am I now trying to win the approval of human beings, or of God? Or am I trying to please people? If I were still trying to please people, I would not be a servant of Christ.

(Galatians 1:10 NIV)

# Day 78

## THOUGHT POWER

........................................

I cannot change you.
But I can change the way I think about you.

Father give me Your perspective...let my thoughts align with Yours.

I cannot change the way you think about me.
But I can change the way I think about the way you think about me.

Father give me Your perspective...let my thoughts align with Yours.

I cannot change my situation.
But I can change the way I think about my situation.

Father give me Your perspective...let my thoughts align with Yours.

This is thought power.

### SELAH!

*Scripture*  So letting your sinful nature control your mind leads to death. But letting the Spirit control your mind leads to life and peace.
(Romans 8:6 NLT)

# Day 79

## ANOTHER BIRTHDAY

..........................................

Time marches on
cake candles celebration...again
grateful for the afterglow of wisdom and life

*Scripture*  All the days ordained for me were written in Your book before one of them came to be. (Psalm 139:16b NIV)

# Day 80

## AN IN SPITE OF PRAISE

........................................

Father God I praise You today.

In spite of my circumstances……I praise You!
In spite of my situation……I praise You!
In the midst of my tears…I praise You!

I push aside worry, hurt, pain, and disappointment to praise You.
I push aside fear, disillusionment, confusion, and despair to praise You.
I push aside my enemies, my haters, my users, and abusers to praise You.
I push aside those who stole from me, lied about me, cheated on me, and maligned my name to praise You.
I push aside those who scorn me, tear me down, wish me ill, and do me wrong to praise You.
Father I push aside everyone and everything to praise You.

You are faithful, loving, gracious, and kind.
You are merciful, just, compassionate, and wise.
You are great, mighty, awesome, powerful, able to do exceedingly abundantly above all I can ask, think, or imagine.
You are the all-knowing, ever-present, slow to anger, excellent, eternal, Holy One.
You are the Alpha and the Omega, the Beginning and the End, the Great I AM, the Ancient of Days.
You O God are the One who spoke and it was, the One who speaks and it is, for when You decree a thing, it is so.
Father God I praise You for who You are.

Father God I praise You today.

You set up governments and rulers and take them down.

You uphold the universe by the Word of Your power.
Your enemies melt like wax in Your presence; they blow away as chaff in the wind.
You sit on Your throne and laugh at them for You know their day is coming and You know their end.

You hold the life of every living creature and the breath of mankind in Your hand.
What other god is like you?
There is none like You.
You are the only true and living God.
There is nothing too hard for You.

So Father God, right now, because of who You are, I exalt You, I extol You, I lift You up, and I magnify Your Holy Name.
I bless You and give You the highest praise…
Hallelujah!
Hallelujah!
Hallelujah!

I praise You for being the great God that You are.
I praise You for loving me.
I praise You for being my Father.
Let Your Kingdom come and Your will be done in me and that which concerns me for Your honor and glory.

Father God I praise You today.
In spite of my circumstances……I praise You.

*Scripture*  *I will bless the Lord at all times: his praise shall continually be in my mouth.* (Psalms 34:1)

## Day 81

### LORD HEAL THE CRACKS IN MY HEART

............................................

Lord heal the cracks in my heart
That only You can see,

Heal the cracks in my heart
I want to be free,

Heal the cracks in my heart
My strength is all gone,

Heal the cracks in my heart
I want to move on.

Lord heal the cracks in my heart.

*Scripture*  *He heals the brokenhearted and binds up their wounds.*
*(Psalms 147:3 NIV)*

# Day 82
## WHAT WILL YOU DO?– JUST CURIOUS

..............................................

Are you going to be the unique, handcrafted masterpiece that God created you to be?
or
Are you going to settle to be a cheap copy of someone else?

What will you do? – Just Curious...
Are you going to discover and follow the unique path that God has marked out for you?
or
Are you going to settle and follow someone else's path?

What will you do? – Just Curious...
Are you going to let God set the pace and rhythm for your life and march to the beat of His drum for you?
or
Are you going to settle to let others set the pace and rhythm for your life and march to the beat of their drum for you?

What will you do? – Just Curious...
Are you going to let God determine the standards, boundaries and potential of your life?
or
Are you going to settle and let the world determine these for you?

What will you do? – Just Curious...
Selah!

*Scripture*   Who, then, are those who fear the Lord? He will instruct them in the ways they should choose.        (Psalms 25:12 NIV)

# Day 83

## FIERY TRIAL

..........................................

Lord as I walk through this fiery trial,
Let me be not afraid,
Let me count it all joy,
Let me be a bush burning but not consumed,
That others may stand in awe of You,
That others may glory in You.

*Scripture*    Beloved, do not think it strange concerning the fiery trial which is to try you, as though some strange thing happened to you; but rejoice to the extent that you partake of Christ's sufferings, that when His glory is revealed, you may also be glad with exceeding joy.      (I Peter 4:12-13 NKJV)

# Day 84

## HARDHEADED BILL

..........................................

His name was William his friends called him Bill,
He was still young, not quite over the hill,
His wife Sue, concerned about his eternal fate,
Pleaded, "Honey please accept the Lord before it's too late".

"I'll get saved later Sue!" Bill sharply said,
His words cut through her spirit and hit her like lead,
"I'm successful, I'm healthy, I'm happy, I'm free,
I will not be tied down by that old drudgery."

So Bill kept on going his own merry way,
He slept, ate, drank, worked and rose up to play,
But little did he know that the next day at four,
The death angel would visit and be knocking at his door.

He awoke early as usual doing his do,
Then sat at the table and had breakfast with Sue,
She held his hand tenderly again expressing her heart,
But to her dismay he wanted absolutely no part.

Bill left home that morning not giving Sue a nod,
Totally annoyed by her obsession with God,
He thought to himself, I'm a hit not a miss,
Why does my wife have to carry on like this?

He entered his office dressed sharp as a tack,
Of compliments and adoring looks there was no lack,
He chaired the board meeting with agility and flair,
And left feeling good with his head in the air.

Walking back to his desk Bill began to feel strange,
It was 3:59, now his world would change.
Like an arrow a searing pain shot through his head,
And at 4:00 pm sharp he collapsed dead.

Bill's coworkers were stunned, full of unbelief,
His wife Sue was laden with unfathomable grief,
How can this be? they all said,
How can a man so alive drop down dead?

The moral of the story is clear as can be,
Bill played around with eternity,
He was hardheaded though he knew what to do,
You've read about him, now what about you?

*Scripture*  *For God so loved the world, that he gave His only begotten Son, that whosoever believeth in Him should not perish, but have everlasting life.* (John 3:16)

[Disclaimer - I do not know, or have never known any persons married to each other by the names of "Bill" and "Sue" so any such occurrence is pure coincidence.]

# Day 85

## ANOTHER WEDDING ANNIVERSARY

........................................

Married twenty-five years
laughter, joy, sadness, tears
thanking God for our time together

*Scripture*  But at the beginning of creation God 'made them male and female.' 'For this reason a man will leave his father and mother and be united to his wife, and the two will become one flesh.' So they are no longer two, but one. Therefore what God has joined together, let man not separate.     (Mark 10:6-9 NIV)

# Day 86
## THE ZONE

........................................

*T*here is a place that I call THE ZONE.

It is a place you enter by determining to submit fully to the Lord in the midst of a difficult circumstance...

It is a place of prioritizing pleasing the Lord above all else, independent of what anyone does or does not do to or for you...

It is a place where the only thing that matters is obeying the Lord and meeting His requirements no matter what transpires...

It is a place of intense trust in the Lord and reliance on Him to call the shots whether or not you understand, agree with, or like what He decides; your views, opinions or feelings have no voting power there...

It is a place of pain to your flesh because when flesh rears its head and wants to take command of your will, flesh must die...

It is a place of intense character formation, spiritual grounding, and maturation...

It is a place of peace, protection, power, grace, and joy, saturated by the presence of God...

It is a place of divine fellowship and favor because your decision to keep the Lord on the seat of the throne of your heart in spite of what happens, or does not happen, greatly pleases Him...

It is a place the enemy despises because he can't touch you there the way he desires to touch you...

It is a place the enemy despises because he can't mess with your mind and your emotions and have you at the point of a nervous breakdown the way he'd like to...

It is a place the enemy despises because his weapons have no true effect there...

It is a place that once into, the enemy desperately wants to get you to step out of so he can pounce on a chance to destroy some aspect of your being...

It is a place that if by some chance under the stress of your circumstances you temporarily step outside of, perhaps in a surge of intense emotions or momentary poor judgment, that it's best to repent and run back into its covering as quickly as you can...

It is a place to never let guilt and condemnation keep you from returning to...

It is a place of supernatural strength for your body, mind, soul, and spirit to endure the most daunting vicissitudes of life...

It is a place of assured victory...

It is a place I call THE ZONE.

*Scripture*   He who dwells in the secret place of the Most High shall abide under the shadow of the Almighty. I will say of the Lord, "He is my refuge and my fortress; my God, in Him I will trust.
(Psalms 91:1-2 NKJV)

# Day 87
## GOSSIP

........................................

Hears
Shares
Cares
Fears
Stares
Jeers
Airs
Tears
Prayers

*Scripture*  A gossip betrays a confidence; so avoid anyone who talks too much.  (Proverbs 20:19 NIV)

# Day 88
## THE QUIET ZONE

### *T*HE
Time out from everything and everyone
Helping others temporarily suspended
Entire being in a state of rest

### QUIET
Quietness is the order of the day
Understood by some...misunderstood by others
Intimate time with God is paramount
Emptying, re-filling, re-shaping, re-energizing, replenishing
Talking with others limited

### ZONE
Zappers of energy kept at bay
Only what God orders is in order
No room for entertaining issues, or stress
Exiting the zone when God's purposes are complete and He gives the green light

### SELAH!

*Scriptures* He said to them, "Come away by yourselves to a secluded place and rest a little while"—for there were many [people who were continually] coming and going, and they could not even find time to eat. (Mark 6:31 AMP)

The Lord is my Shepherd [to feed, to guide and to shield me], I shall not want. He lets me lie down in green pastures; He leads me beside the still and quiet waters. He refreshes and restores my soul (life); He leads me in the paths of righteousness for His name's sake. (Psalms 23:1-3 AMP)

# Day 89
## STILL WAITING

..............................................

Still waiting to ...

Still waiting for...

Still waiting on...

Be patient

Be faithful

Be prayerful

Be grateful

Your time will come!

SELAH!

*Scriptures*  He hath made every thing beautiful in his time.
(Ecclesiastes 3:11)

*The Lord is my portion and my inheritance," says my soul;
"Therefore I have hope in Him and wait expectantly for Him."
The Lord is good to those who wait [confidently] for Him, To
those who seek Him [on the authority of God's word]. It is good
that one waits quietly for the salvation of the Lord.*
(Lamentations 3:24-26 AMP)

# Day 90

## CAN I HAVE SOME TIME WITH YOU?

..............................................

Hello.
Can I have your attention?

No, no, not out there.
In here.
Yes, in here.
I live in you..., remember...or have you been so busy that you've forgotten that?

Listen.

Can I have some time with you?
Just Me and you.
No one else.
No-thing else.
Just Me and you.

I have some things to tell you.
I have some things to show you.
I have some directions to give you.

There are some longings in you I'd like to fulfill.
There is some inner-healing I'd like to complete.
There are some things in your life I want to restore, rejuvenate, revive, make whole.
There is another level of peace, power, and purpose I want to manifest in and through you.

Can I have some time with you?
I'd really like to have some time with you.

Hello!
Do I have your attention?......I felt you backing away.
Listen.

Slow down.
Reduce the pace.
Quiet yourself.
Settle yourself.
Turn down the volume.
Shut off the streams.
Block out the voices.
Get away from the clutter.
Lay it all down.
Carve out the time.
Come to Me.

I'll be waiting for you.
I'll be waiting just for you.

Can I have some time with you?
I'd really like some time with you.

Selah!

*Scripture* *You will show me the path of life; in Your presence is fullness of joy; at Your right hand are pleasures forevermore.* (Psalm 16:11)

# Day 91

## LORD CALM THE RAGING STORM

Lord calm the raging storm in me,
The one that no one else can see,
This is not the way I want to be,
Just say the word and I'll be free.

*Scripture*    *And he arose, and rebuked the wind, and said unto the sea, Peace, be still. And the wind ceased, and there was a great calm.* (Mark 4:39)

# Day 92

## BROTHER GEORGE & PEARLINE

..............................................

Brother George got up, stretched and rubbed his eyes,
Tonight I wonder which girl will be my prize,
Some of them are so weak they can't resist me,
One compliment, one dinner, and they dish it for free.

He sat on the bed and got out his black book,
He flipped through the pages to take a quick look,
Not Sister Donna, not Sister Marsha, not Lucy, not Clem,
Man they ain't no challenge I've already run through them.

Then Brother George remembered Pearline the new lady next door,
Low-cut blouse, skin-tight pants hey, who could ask for more,
Oh man she sooo sexy, I just can't wait
So he got dressed, went over and asked her for a date.

"Sure" Pearline said with a smile on her face,
Then she slipped on an outfit and they left her place,
But what Brother George did not realize,
There was much more to Pearline than what met his eyes.

After having dinner and now sitting on the beach,
Brother George grinned to himself, "Now my prize is in reach",
So he gently began to stroke Pearline's hand,
And next thing you know they were rolling in the sand.

He took Pearline home and gave her a good night kiss,
Thinking, "Man I didn't expect it to be as easy as this",
Back in his bedroom he puffed up his chest,
and said, "Boy, George you bad now, that's another conquest."

Two days later Brother George's cousin stopped by,
Brother George told him about Pearline and he started to sigh,
He said, "Boy I hope you're not talking about that woman next door"
"Because she has AIDS" – Brother George fell to the floor!

When Brother George's cousin left he could not sleep,
"But she looks so healthy this really is deep",
From the outside he did not notice one thing,
And now he sorrowfully regretted having the fling.

Months later to the doctor Brother George went shaking,
When called in for his test results his knees were quaking,
The doctor looked at him and sadly shook his head,
"I'm sorry except for a miracle you'll soon be dead".

Brother George went and found Pearline, his heart filled with dread,
"Girl you know you had AIDS", he angrily said,
Pearline shrugged her shoulders without batting an eye,
"Well you wanted me, right?", was her reply.

Pearline died first then Brother George followed her,
Leaving their families and friends in a blur,
It's sad to say but the truth is you see,
What happened to them is a common story.

Many, many a life have been lost this way,
Because from God's guidelines we go astray,
No, I sit not in judgment, all pious and scorning,
But as one that's concerned and simply issuing us all a warning.

*Scripture*   *Run from sexual sin! No other sin so clearly affects the body as this one does. For sexual immorality is a sin against your own body.*
(1 Corinthians 6:18 NLT)

[Disclaimer: I do not know, or have never known any persons by the names of "Brother George" or "Pearline" who had, or have, any kind of relationship with each other so any such occurrence is pure coincidence.]

# Day 93

## TIME FOR A RE-THINK

............................................

Colli-shun
transit-shun
reposit-shun

Selah!

*Scripture*  For my thoughts are not your thoughts, neither are your ways my ways, says the Lord. For as the heavens are higher than the earth, so are my ways higher than your ways and my thoughts than your thoughts. (Isaiah 55:8-9 AMPC)

## Day 94

### ANOTHER CASUALTY OF INFIDELITY

*Enticing visual delight*
*calculatingly stealthily crossing boundaries*
*stolen waters sweet?*

*lies, deceit, trust crushed,*
*drenching tears, lost years, confusion, fears,*
*another casualty of infidelity.*

*Scriptures* So, if you think you are standing firm, be careful that you don't fall! No temptation has overtaken you except what is common to mankind. And God is faithful; he will not let you be tempted beyond what you can bear. But when you are tempted, he will also provide a way out so that you can endure it.
(1 Corinthians 10:12-13 NIV)

*Give honor to marriage, and remain faithful to one another in marriage. God will surely judge people who are immoral and those who commit adultery.* (Hebrews 13:4 NLT)

# Day 95
## A PATH TO THE PROMISE

........................................

*S*ituation

A promise from God

Excitement
Hope
Joy
Obedience
Worship
Time

Opposite circumstances
Attack of doubt
Remembering the promise
Holding fast to the promise

Faith
Hope
Obedience
Worship
Time
Time

More opposite circumstances
Greater attack of doubt
Remembering the promise
Reminding God of the promise
Holding fast to the promise
Clinging to the promise

Faith
Hope
Strength
Obedience
Worship
Praise

Time
Time
Time

Remembering the promise
Holding fast to the promise
Clinging to the promise

Faith
Hope
Obedience
Worship
Praise

Time
Time
Time
Time

Weariness

Remembering the promise
Reminding God of the promise
Holding fast to the promise
Clinging to the promise

Faith
Hope
Obedience
Worship
Praise

Time

Manifestation

Joy
Thanksgiving
Praise
Glory to God

*Scripture*  *God is not a man, that He should lie, nor a son of man, that He should repent. Has He said, and will He not do? Or has He spoken, and will He not make it good?* (Numbers 23:19 NKJV)

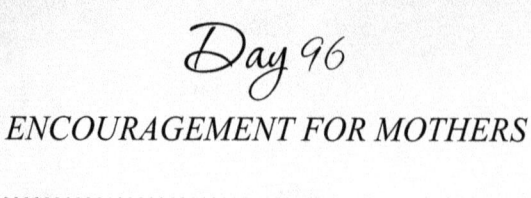

## ENCOURAGEMENT FOR MOTHERS

..............................................

### M – Militant
When the enemy attacks, do not fear.
Do not cower down.
Rise up in faith, engage your spiritual weapons and fight for the souls of your children.
Remember you are more than a conqueror through Christ Jesus and greater is He that is in you than he that is in the world.

### O – Overflowing with Love
Love your children always and remember that love also entails engaging discipline, setting boundaries and withholding some things for their own good.

### T – Trust God
No matter how bad a situation seems, remember you serve an awesome mighty, powerful, loving, wise, just, and holy God, who sees and knows all about everything you encounter and who is well able to do exceedingly abundantly above and beyond anything you can ask, think or even imagine. Trust Him.

### H – Hear and Obey the Holy Spirit
Remember that the Holy Spirit is the greatest teacher and counselor when it comes to parenting your children. Hear and obey His wisdom and instruction as revealed in the Word and spoken to your heart.

### E – Endurance
When things get rough, don't give up. Hang on in there knowing that His grace is sufficient and this too shall pass.

## R – Rest

Make sure your mind, body, soul and spirit get adequate rest; the world won't fall apart if you take some time to nurture yourself. Remember you are not superwoman and you do have limits; honor that and don't let the enemy deceive you into believing otherwise and thereby gain a foothold in your life to break you down.

Selah!

*Scripture*  *May the Lord give you increase more and more, you and your children.* (Psalm 115:14 NKJV)

## Day 97
### HOPE FOR THE SUICIDAL

························································

So many bad decisions.
So many stupid mistakes.
So many empty relationships.
So many failures.

So many times of saying I'll never do it again, only to do it again.

So many broken promises.
So many lost opportunities.
So many dashed hopes.
So many pointless dreams.
So many disappointments.

So much abuse.
So much rejection.
So much heartache.
So much discouragement.
So much pain.

So much darkness.
So much bondage.
So much aloneness.

Tears, tears.
Where can I turn?
Tears, lots of tears.

Who can help me?
Desperation.
There's no one here.
Desperation.

I can't take this anymore.
Despair.

What's the point?
Deep despair.

I may as well end it all.
Deeper despair.

My life does not matter.
Utter despair.

I will end it all.

"Jesus."
"Jesus."

Why is this name coming to my mind?

"Jesus."
"Jesus."
"Jesus."

Why do I keep hearing "Jesus"?

Who is Jesus?
Who?
Who?
Wait.

I vaguely remember overhearing Paula talking to Steve during lunch last week about this guy called Jesus.

Yes, I vaguely remember her saying something like this Jesus was the Son of God and He loved people so much He gave His life for them.

It's kind of coming back.
Now I remember.

She said that this Jesus guy was the Son of God and He came down from heaven to earth and died on a cross to pay the price for all the bad stuff or sin people have done and then He rose from the dead and whoever believes this can have eternal life and a future with Him.

She said if you believe this, Jesus will wash all your sins away and you will be a new creation and have a new beginning, and God knows I need a new beginning.

Paula sounded so convinced of this stuff.

Maybe I need this Jesus.
Maybe I should call on him.
What do I have to lose?

"Jesus."
"Jesus."
Jesus, can you hear me?
If you're real please help me.

Please come and lift me out of this dark pit.
Please forgive me of my sins.
Please cleanse me.
Please heal me.

Please break these chains from off of my life.
Please mend the shattered pieces of my heart.
Please restore hope in me.
Please give me a reason to live.
Please come to me.
Please touch me.

I believe you can.
Somehow I know you can.
Please touch me now and I know I'll be free.
Please do it for me.
I know you can do it for me.

Wait.

Something just happened.
Something really happened.

The weight.
The heaviness.
The darkness.
It's gone!

It's all gone!
It's really gone!
I feel so light!
I feel so pure!
I feel so clean!

You are real!
You are really real!
And you must love me!
You must really love me!
You've set me free!
I'm free!
I'm free!

Thank you...Thank you!

I'm free!
I'm finally free!
Thank you Jesus!

I am so glad I did not end my life!
Suicide is not the answer!
Jesus You're the answer!

I have new life!
I have new joy!
I have new hope!
I have new peace!

I am free!
I am finally free!

*Scripture*   *If the Son therefore shall make you free, ye shall be free indeed.*
*(John 8:36)*

# Day 98
## LORD WHEN IT COMES TO PRAYER HERE'S THE DEAL

Lord, when it comes to prayer, here's the deal...

I'll decide when I want to talk to You.

Off the top, I'm not a morning person so getting up early in the morning is out of the question...I need my sleep.

I work during the day so that's not a good time to talk to You either...I have important conversations to hold with my colleagues, clients, business partners and associates...and in between I need to talk with my friends, family, and my special boo...You understand.

At night I gotta do the family thing and catch up with my online crew, you know, the people I'm in touch with on Facebook, Twitter, LinkedIn, WhatsApp, Instagram and Snapchat...and I need to complete my course assignment, exercise, eat, plus get in some TV and catch up on the news...things are tight at night.

So Lord as You can see, I'm busy so I'll decide when I can fit You in.

But don't get me wrong now Lord, when I say fit You in, I don't want You to think I mean any long drawn out thing.

Whatever I ask You for, just give it to me, and don't take long...

If I have a problem and ask You to take care of it, do it right away...If I ask You to heal someone, just heal them...I ain't into this tarrying thing or whatever they call it...You say You can do anything so just do it...no need to draw this out.

And another thing, don't expect me to shut myself in any room alone at any time and pray to You...all that ain't necessary...we can talk on the run, that's more convenient.

And just in case You're thinking about it, when I pray to You, don't switch on me and turn around and ask me to pray about anyone or anything…I really ain't on that run! I only pray about what directly concerns me… everyone can pray for themselves and their own stuff.

Oh, and one more thing, about these church prayer meetings, don't bother to ask because I won't be going to any…being around a bunch of people running on and on and crying and wailing and speaking in that weird, freaky language, I ain't for that! Me and You talking, that's cool…that's definitely enough.

So Lord, that's the deal!

Is this what your life says to God when it comes to prayer?
Be honest…does any of this resonate with you?

If so, let today be your day to repent and make any needed change.

Selah!

*Scriptures* With all prayer and petition pray [with specific requests] at all times [on every occasion and in every season] in the Spirit, and with this in view, stay alert with all perseverance and petition [interceding in prayer] for all God's people.
(Ephesians 6:18 AMP)

*Be unceasing and persistent in prayer.*
(1 Thessalonians 5:17 AMP)

# Day 99
## THIS CHRISTMAS

This Christmas,
each time you see a light, remember that Jesus is the light of the world.

This Christmas,
each time you see a gift, remember that God gave the greatest gift in sending His only begotten Son to earth so that whoever believes in Him shall not perish but have everlasting life.

This Christmas,
each time you see a Christmas tree, remember the price Jesus paid for your salvation by suffering and dying on the cross.

This Christmas,
each time you see preparations made in commemoration and celebration of the first arrival of our Lord and Savior Jesus Christ, remember the importance of preparing yourself for His next arrival because He is coming again, not as a baby in a manger, but as a mighty, conquering King.

This Christmas,
may you and your loved ones have a blessed, peaceful, safe, and Christ-filled, holiday and remember that Jesus is the reason for the season.

*Scripture*   For a child is born to us, a son is given to us. The government will rest on his shoulders. And he will be called: Wonderful Counselor, Mighty God, Everlasting Father, Prince of Peace. His government and its peace will never end. He will rule with fairness and justice from the throne of his ancestor David for all eternity. The passionate commitment of the Lord of Heaven's Armies will make this happen! (Isaiah 9:6-7 NLT)

## Day 100
### THIS YEAR MAY YOUR CHRISTMAS BE...

••••••••••••••••••••••••••••••••••••••••••••

This year may your Christmas be:

**C**hrist-filled not **C**hrist-less
**H**eavenly not **H**ellish
**R**elaxing not **R**ushed
**I**nspiring not **I**nfuriating
**S**mooth not **S**trained
**T**ranquil not **T**ense
**M**erry not **M**orose
**A**wesome not **A**wful
**S**anctified not **S**inful

A lot will depend on your attitude, perspective and choices.

Selah!

*Scripture:* For a child is born to us, a son is given to us. The government will rest on his shoulders. And he will be called: Wonderful Counselor, Mighty God, Everlasting Father, Prince of Peace. His government and its peace will never end. He will rule with fairness and justice from the throne of his ancestor David for all eternity. The passionate commitment of the Lord of Heaven's Armies will make this happen! (Isaiah 9:6-7 NLT)

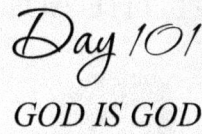
## GOD IS GOD

• • • • • • • • • • • • • • • • • • • • • • • • • • • • • • • • • • • • • • • •

God is God.
He is who He is.
He is all of who He is.
We cannot reject parts of Him yet claim to accept Him.
He cannot be separated from Himself.

We cannot accept His attributes we find comfortable pleasing and beneficial,
yet reject those we find sobering, daunting and commanding of reverential fear.

We cannot accept that He is a God of love, mercy and grace,
yet reject that He is also a God of holiness, judgment and wrath.

God is God.
He is who He is.
He is all of who He is.
We cannot reject parts of Him yet claim to accept Him.
He cannot be separated from Himself.

**SELAH!**

*Scriptures* *The Lord is gracious and compassionate, slow to anger and rich in love.* (Psalms 145:8 NIV)

*But just as he who called you is holy, so be holy in all you do; for it is written: "Be holy, because I am holy."* (1 Peter 1:15-16 NIV)

*The Lord reigns forever; he has established his throne for judgment.* (Psalms 9:7 NIV)

# About the Author

Kim L. Sweeting is a Christ follower, wife, mother, minister, Certified Life Coach, counselor, writer, and blogger whose passion is to communicate with people in ways that will help them grow spiritually, develop personally, and live effectively, according to God's purpose, plans and principles in all areas of their lives. She resides in beautiful Nassau, Bahamas with her husband, three children, four adopted dogs and adopted cat, and worships at Family of Faith Ministries International where she serves on the leadership team.

www.ingramcontent.com/pod-product-compliance
Lightning Source LLC
Chambersburg PA
CBHW060534100426
42743CB00009B/1525